Also by Corey Green:

Finding Karate

Karate Wise: A Technical Guide to Teaching Self-Defense

Stories From The Driver's Seat: 1,000 rides in 100 days.

IMPROBABLE

The Story of

Corey Green and **Green's Karate**

Improbable

Written by Corey Green

First Edition

Published in the United States of America

ISBN: [Insert ISBN]

Cover design by Corey Green
Interior design by Corey Green

— IMPROBABLESTORY.COM —
The Story Continues

For information regarding permissions, speaking engagements, or future publications, visit:
www.ImprobableStory.com

The events described in this memoir are true to the best of the author's recollection. Some names, identifying details, and conversations may have been condensed or reconstructed from memory to improve readability while preserving the substance and intent of the events described.

Printed in the United States of America.

To God, who continued writing chapters long after I thought the story was over.

"Blessed is the one who perseveres under trial because, having stood the test, that person will receive the crown of life that the Lord has promised to those who love him."

— James 1:12

"Let us not become weary in doing good, for at the proper time we will reap a harvest if we do not give up."

— Galatians 6:9

Contents

REFLECTION

People see the school.

The medals.

The success stories.

What they do not see is everything underneath it.

The wilderness.
The fear.
The bullying.
The losses.

The moments that almost broke me.

Or the long road that somehow led here.

People have asked me for years how all of this happened.
The truth is…

I have been trying to understand it myself.

Because when I look back at my life, there are moments that still feel impossible.

Moments that should have ended differently.

Moments that changed everything.

And somehow, against the odds, I kept moving forward.

This is that story.

PROLOGUE
THE CHARGING BEAR

My first memory of life is a bear.

Not school. Not a toy. Not a birthday.

A bear.

I was three years old living in Beluga, Alaska.

Most people have never heard of Beluga. Back then there were maybe thirty people there. No neighborhoods. No traffic lights. No stores down the road. Just wilderness, snow, airplanes, and whatever nature decided to do that day.

I had just come out of the shower and walked toward the window when I saw something moving in the distance.

I only said one word.

"Bear."

My oldest brother stepped beside me and looked out the window.
"Dad," he said calmly, "there's a bear out there."

Everyone in the house turned.

About a thousand feet away stood a massive brown bear.

My father didn't hesitate.
He walked straight to the gun wall, grabbed his shotgun, and turned toward us.

"Go to the back bedroom," he said. "Grab the spotlight. Shine it on the bear so I have something to shoot at."

We ran.

When the light hit the animal, its eyes reflected back bright red against the darkness.

I can still see them.

The bear lifted its head.

Sniffed the air.

Then it charged.

Everything changed instantly.

The bear came straight toward my father, covering ground fast.
He raised the shotgun and fired.

The first shot hit its front leg.

The bear dive rolled.
Then got back up.

And kept coming.

Now it was close.

Close enough that even as a three-year-old I knew this was different.

My father waited.

Raised the gun again.

Fired.

The second shot hit the bear in the heart.

It dropped instantly.

For a moment, nobody moved.

I stood there looking through the window trying to understand what I had just seen.
The red eyes.
The spotlight.
The sound of the shotgun.
The snow.

The silence afterward.

That became the first memory of my life.

I did not understand what it was building yet.

Looking back now, it feels strangely appropriate.

Because my life would become filled with moments where danger appeared without warning.

Avalanches.
Storms.
Accidents.
Near misses.
Loss.
Reinvention.

And somehow, over and over again,

I kept moving forward.

I just didn't know it yet.

At three years old, all I knew was this:

There had been a bear outside.

And my story had already begun.

The Long Road North

Before my story began, my parents had already made a decision that would shape the rest of my life.

In 1976, my family left Tallahassee, Florida and began driving north in a motorhome toward a place most people only saw on maps.
Alaska.

Inside that motorhome were my three older brothers, my mother, and my father. It was a long journey across thousands of miles of highway, through states and landscapes that must have changed dramatically as they moved farther north.

At the time I wasn't even born yet, but that journey became the first chapter of the life I would eventually grow into.

My father had been offered work through the IBEW, the International Brotherhood of Electrical Workers. The opportunity pulled my parents toward Alaska, a place known for hard work, harsh winters, and opportunities that didn't exist in many other parts of the country.

Eventually the family arrived in Anchorage, where I was born.
Not long after that, another opportunity appeared.
My father was offered a job in a small community called Beluga and when I was about eleven months old, our family moved there.

Beluga wasn't the kind of place most people imagine when they think about growing up. It was remote, surrounded by wilderness, and shaped by the realities of life in Alaska.
That was where my earliest years unfolded.

From the time I was almost one year old until nearly seven, Beluga was home. Those years were filled with the sights and sounds of Alaska - open land, cold winters, wildlife, and the quiet that comes with living in a place where nature is always present.

I didn't know it at the time, but growing up in that environment was teaching me lessons that would stay with me for the rest of my life.

Lessons about awareness. About resilience.
About how small human beings really are in a landscape that powerful.

Eventually our family moved back toward Anchorage and by the time I turned seven years old, something happened that would change the direction of my life in a completely different way.

I saw a movie.

It was The Karate Kid.

Like millions of kids who watched that film, I was fascinated.
The story of a young kid learning martial arts, finding discipline, and gaining confidence struck something inside me. I saw it at our house and became instantly inspired. I didn't know it yet, but that movie had just planted the first seed of what would become a lifelong journey.

Beluga would become home. I did not know it yet, but it would also become the place where my first great fear found me.

Devil Outside

About a year after the bear, winter had returned to Beluga.

One night my family gathered in the living room watching Halloween II on our floor-model twenty-seven-inch Sony television. I sat on the couch beside the window, half watching the movie, half staring into the dark outside.

My father eventually said he was tired and went to bed in the back room. The movie kept playing. My brothers and my mom stayed focused on the screen. I wasn't really interested in the movie anyway.

Then something moved in the corner of my eye.

Outside, maybe thirty feet from the house, a figure was walking slowly in circles in the snow. I tried to get everyone's attention.

"Hey… someone's outside."

They were too caught up in the movie.

"Shut up, Bucky."

So I stopped talking.

I thought, "Fine they'll figure it out."

Then a ring of fire appeared in the snow.

Everyone noticed that.

People rushed to the window.

The figure walked through the flames as if nothing was there.

And then it walked toward the house.

Closer.

Closer.

When the face came into the window light it looked exactly like the red-horned devil you see in cartoons.

Panic spread through the room.

"The front door!"

My brothers ran to lock it just as banging started.

Then someone yelled,

"The back door!"

They ran again and barely got that one locked before the banging moved there too.

For a moment everything went silent.

Then someone said,

"Where's Dad?"

His bed was empty.

The devil came back to the front door and started pounding again.

I dove under the old couch in the middle of the living room.

My brothers decided to open the door.

The devil walked straight across the room toward me.
It reached under the couch, grabbed me and started shaking me while I cried.

Then the lights came on.

The mask came off.

It was my father.

Later he hung the devil mask on a wooden two by four at the entrance to his workshop at the back of the cabin so I would see it every time I passed by.

And every time I saw it, I felt the same thing again.

Fear.

GRANDPA HUBBARD

Spring eventually came back to Beluga.

The snow began to soften, the light stayed longer in the sky, and one day my grandfather arrived to visit us in the little cabin.

His name was Claudis Arza Hubbard. He was also known as Grandpa Hubbard.

He stayed with us only a short time, but the things he said stayed with me much longer.

Grandpa talked to me about Jesus.

I was only four years old, so I didn't understand everything he explained, but I remember the calm way he spoke about faith and about trying to live a good life.

At one point I asked him something that had been bothering me.
"Grandpa, why does Grandma always forget my name?"

My nickname was Bucky, and sometimes when we visited she didn't remember it.

Grandpa paused for a moment and then said something I had never heard before.

"She has something called Alzheimer's."

I asked him what that meant. and
he explained it in the simplest way he could.
"It's when someone begins to forget their past."
I remember standing there, four years old, thinking about that.

For some reason that idea struck me deeply.

Forgetting your past.

In that moment I made a quiet promise to myself.

Don't forget your past.

Some memories fade.
Others become the foundation you stand on.

Right then I started thinking about everything I could remember.

The bear. The snow. The cabin.

The things that had already happened in my life.
I didn't know it then, but that promise to remember would follow me for the rest of my life.

Constant Cold / Isolation / Survival Atmosphere

Beluga was different than anything most people could probably imagine.

Maybe thirty people at the time.

Nothing but woods, snow, silence, and cold.

Real cold.

Most of my memories were wilderness, survival, fear, snow, and trying to understand the world I was growing up in.

Looking back now, Beluga almost feels less like a town and more like another planet.

It was a place that taught respect.

Flying Back and Forth To Anchorage For Food

One of the strangest parts about growing up in Beluga was how normal flying became.

Most people grow up getting into a car to buy groceries.

We got into airplanes.

We would fly back and forth to Anchorage for food and supplies because there was no real store nearby.

As a little kid, I became conscious very early that airplanes were simply part of survival.

The sounds of the planes, the vibration, the weather, and rough landings all became normal life.

Anchorage felt massive.

Beluga felt isolated.

At the time I didn't think much about it.

It was simply our life.

Walking on Winter

It was one of the coldest days I can remember.

The temperature had dropped to around minus eighty degrees, and a few feet of snow had fallen in the previous day or two.

Outside the cabin everything was frozen solid, the kind of cold that made people stay bundled inside where it was warm.

But I noticed something different.

The snow had formed a thick crust across the surface.
It looked like a white sheet stretched across the landscape.

And I realized something.
I was small enough, light enough, that I might be able to walk on top of it.
To a kid weighing maybe forty pounds, it felt like a once-in-a-lifetime opportunity.

I asked my mom if I could go outside.

"No," she said immediately. "It's too cold. You'll freeze."

I kept pleading. "Just one minute."

She hesitated, knowing how dangerous the cold was.
She explained that at temperatures like that my hands could freeze in seconds, and breathing the air too long could hurt my lungs.

But she also understood what I was asking.

Finally she agreed.

"Just one minute."

So I stepped outside.

The air was brutal, the kind that stings your face the moment it touches you.

But when I stepped onto the snow something incredible happened.

It held.
The crust didn't break.

For a moment I could go anywhere.

The entire white landscape was like a frozen floor stretching out in every direction.

It felt like walking on top of winter itself.

Yes, it was dangerously cold.

But for that brief moment it was also amazing.

A chance of a lifetime.

The Tree

Winter in Beluga meant snow machines.
Not snowmobiles.
In Alaska, everyone called them snow machines.

One day my brothers and I were riding behind my father on sleds.

Each of us had our own bright orange plastic sled tied to the back of the machine with ropes.

My dad was driving in a huge arc around the yard, pulling us behind him like a train of sleds sliding across the snow.

We were all leaning into the turns like race car drivers.

The best way I can describe it now is that we were moving around the yard like NASCAR drivers, circling in the same direction.

I happened to be riding the outside lane.
The far right.

That's when the turn got wider.

And wider.

Until suddenly I realized where I was headed.

A tree.

Before I could do anything, my sled shot straight into it.

Head first.

Everything went black for a moment.

Looking back now, it might have been a concussion but at the time I remembered the sudden silence and the strange feeling that everything had stopped.

Then the world slowly came back again.

Snow.

Cold air.

And the realization that I had just slammed head-first into a tree.

Life can change in a second.
Sometimes all othat separates a story from a tragedy is timing.

The Ice Rink

When I was about five years old, my father did something that felt almost magical at the time:

He built us our own ice-skating rink outside the cabin.

In Beluga, winter gave you all the ingredients you needed.

The cold air froze everything solid, and with a little work you could turn a patch of ground into smooth ice.

My father flooded the area with water and let it freeze.

Before long we had a homemade skating rink right outside our house.

That's where I learned what ice skating was.

Years later, when people talked about ice skating after movies like The Karate Kid came out, I always smiled a little.

Because I was already learning to skate two years before the Karate Kid movie existed, out on a homemade rink in a tiny village in Alaska.

It was just another small moment in Beluga.

But for a kid growing up there, it felt like the world.

The Short Fuse

My father was a man who could do almost anything with his hands.

He worked as a lineman for the International Brotherhood of Electrical Workers, and the work paid well.

It was dangerous work too, climbing poles and dealing with power lines in the harsh conditions of Alaska.

He was also a builder.

The cabin we lived in at Beluga wasn't something he bought.
He built it himself.

He knew auto mechanics, construction, electrical work.

Whatever needed to be done, he could usually figure it out.

But he also had something else.
A very short fuse.

One day he was riding his motorcycle down the dirt road near the cabin.

Something happened and he flew over the handlebars.

He hit the ground hard and came back covered in dirt. He had a mouthfull of dirt too.

You could tell he was furious.

Instead of cooling down, he walked the motorcycle back to the cabin.

I watched as he poured gasoline over the bike.

Then he lit it on fire.

Just like that.

The flames rose up around the machine as if it had personally offended him.
That was my father.

A man capable of building a home from the ground up.

A man brave enough to face danger.

But also a man whose anger could burn just as quickly as gasoline.

Riding Ol' Blue

Beluga didn't have much.

There was a small dirt airstrip where planes landed, and that's where the gas pump was.

No convenience store.
No soda machine.
No snacks.

Just a pump sitting there by itself.

And the gas didn't cost anything.

One day we drove our 1977 light blue pickup truck, the one we called Ol' Blue, over to the airstrip to fill up.

After the tank was full my dad suggested something that would never be allowed in most places.

"Ya'll take a ride on top."

So we, my brothers and I climbed up onto the cab of the truck.

We lined up across the roof and laid on our stomachs so we could hold on.

I remember being the second one from the left.

The metal roof felt cold under my chest.

Then the truck started moving.

The wind rushed past us as the truck rolled down the dirt road.

I turned my head and looked at my brothers.

We were all smiling.

No seat belts.

No rules.

Just the sound of the wind and the open Alaska landscape around us.

At the time we had no idea how rare that moment really was.

I remember the bond that my brothers and to us at that time, it was just another afternoon.

But looking back now, it felt almost magical.

For a few minutes we were just kids riding the wind on top of a truck called Ol' Blue.

FORD

The Cliff

It was the Fourth of July, and I was five years old and
we had driven to the top of a cliff to shoot off fireworks.

From up there you could see a long stretch of land and sky, and for a kid it felt like being on top of the world.

I was doing the simple things kids do at that age.

Running around.

Watching the fireworks.

Enjoying the night.

My favorite that evening were the little firecracker tanks that rolled forward and popped as they moved.

Everything felt normal.

Then suddenly my father grabbed me.

He picked me up by my left arm and left leg and started swinging me around.

At first I didn't even understand what was happening.

But then I saw how close we were to the edge of the cliff.

He swung me around again and said something that I will never forget.
"Maybe I should just toss him off this cliff."

I had done nothing wrong.

I remember the fear rising in my chest as he swung me again, this time even closer to the edge.

For a moment it felt like it might actually happen.
Then he stopped.

He didn't throw me.

But something else changed that evening.

Up until then, my father had been the man who stopped the bear.

The man who built our cabin. My father, who could do almost anything.

After that moment and other moments, I felt something different.

Fear.

And the trust I had in him as a child never fully came back.

I was too young to understand why he had done it.

I still don't know the reason.

But that was the day I realized that sometimes the people who are supposed to protect you can also be the ones who scare you the most.

Bush Plane Landing

When supplies ran low in Beluga, it meant it was time to fly.

Oren Hudson was our pilot. A legend of the sky.

The plane I remember most clearly was a Cessna 185 Skywagon.
White, with two wide dark blue stripes running down the side and blue markings on the tail.

When the door opened, the smell hit first.

Old aviation fuel.

Cold metal.
Worn leather seats.
I always tried to get the window seat as soon as I could walk.

As the engine roared to life, the plane rattled and bounced across the strip before lifting into the sky.

From the window I watched the village shrink beneath us.

Snow-covered trees.

Frozen rivers.

Miles of wilderness stretching farther than I could see.

For nine months of the year, that little plane was our road to the outside world.

Once every couple of weeks, sometimes once a month, we flew to Anchorage for supplies. And when we landed in the snow, you could hear it beneath us.

Crunchy at first...
Then squishy as the plane rolled along.

That sound meant we had made it.

At the time, it all felt normal.

Looking back now, I realize how improbable that childhood really was.

In The Garden with God

By the time I was six years old, life in Beluga had already given me a collection of memories that most kids never experience.
There were moments of freedom and adventure, but there were also moments where things went wrong.

I remember one accident where I hit the ground hard enough that everything went blurry for a while. I was at the top of some stairs in the cabin in my pajamas, I thought I was Superman, I fell about 10 feet. When I landed on my right arm, it hurt so badly afterward that I thought it might have been broken. My parents wrapped it up in a ace bandage and called it a day.

Sometimes, as a kid, you didn't always know exactly what had happened.

You just knew you were hurt, and eventually you kept going.

But the memory that stayed with me most from my childhood happened outside near the garden.

I was alone, standing among the plants and dirt, thinking about everything that had already happened in my life.

The bear.
The strange night with the mask.
The things I didn't fully understand yet.

My grandfather had talked to me earlier about Jesus and about faith.

Those ideas were still in my mind.

So at six years old I did the simplest thing a kid could do.

I talked to God.
I didn't know if anyone was listening.
I didn't know if I was doing it the right way.
I just spoke the thoughts that were in my head.
When you're a child growing up in a remote place like Beluga, you spend a lot of time alone with your thoughts.

Sometimes those moments feel bigger than the world around you.

Standing in that little garden, I remember feeling something calm for the first time in a while.

Not answers.

Just a quiet feeling that maybe someone was listening.

At age 6, I knew God was listening. I could feel HIM in my heart.

Soldotna

My father had saved enough money working for the electrical union, IBEW, that we were able to move from Beluga to the next place in our lives.

The king salmon fishing capital of the world.
Soldotna, Alaska.

By the time we moved there, a local fisherman named Les Anderson had not caught what is still considered the largest king salmon ever recorded.

We arrived one year before he accomplished this incredible feat.

Nearly one hundred pounds.

A monster.

Fishing was a way of life there.

Everyone talked about it.

Years later, when I was thirteen, I caught a king salmon that weighed about half that size.

My mom actually caught one four pounds larger than mine just four hours earlier.

But when we first arrived in Soldotna, fishing records and rivers weren't the things that impressed me most.

It was our house. Our new-to-us home.

To me, it felt like a mansion.

It sat at the very top of the hill.

The highest house around.
A tall A-frame wooden house, three stories high with four bedrooms and three bathrooms.

There was already a deck across the front of the house, and we built two more decks ourselves on the sides.

My parents bedroom even had a third-story balcony.

At one point we had seven televisions., seven vehicles and
seven landline telephones.

We were what people would call upper middle class, but as a kid I had absolutely no idea that was our economic status.

It was just normal life.

Then school started.

I was six and three-quarters years old.

Technically I was too old for kindergarten, so the school wanted to test me in reading and math before deciding where to place me.

My brothers had been homeschooled out in the Alaskan bush, and I had been as well to some degree.
Spelling came easily to me.

I remember spelling the word elephant faster than my brother when I was five years old and he was nine.

During the testing, one of the questions showed a picture of a tree.

"How many apples do you see?" the woman asked.

I looked at the picture.

"Nine," I said.

She looked at my hands.

"How did you do that without using your fingers?"

"I used my brain," I answered.

They were considering placing me directly into second grade, but there was one problem.

I was one month too young.

Looking back now, I sometimes wonder how much of my life might have changed if that one month had been different.

Welcome to
Soldotna

Bucky

My nickname was Bucky.

My middle name is Buck.

That name would follow me for years.

The bullying started almost immediately.

At first it was jokes., then more jokes, then humiliation, then survival.

From age six until around fourteen years old I was bullied constantly over my name and being different. Different because I was not good at communicating with others due to isolation in Beluga.

Some people do not understand what years of bullying does to a kid psychologically.

Especially when it becomes daily life.

You begin anticipating humiliation before it even happens.

School stopped feeling like a place to learn and started feeling like something to survive.

I was already socially behind from growing up in Beluga with almost no social interaction through my earliest years.

Then suddenly I was thrown into a school environment where weakness was immediately noticed.

I became extremely aware of people.

Their reactions, laughter, and tone.
Everything.
The bullying slowly started shaping how I viewed myself.

By the time I was 14, there were moments I became borderline suicidal.

I do not say that dramatically.
It is just the truth.

Most people around me probably had no idea how bad things were becoming internally.

But that period would eventually become one of the biggest reasons I later connected with kids that felt isolated, different, rejected, neurodiverse, bullied, or overlooked.

At the time though, I was just trying to survive childhood.

Years later, Buc-ee's would become one of the most recognizable brands in America. Funny how a name I once wished I could escape eventually became something people smiled about.

Bucky Green

Karate Changes Everything

I was around age seven when I saw The Karate Kid movie.

That movie changed my life forever.

At almost the exact same time I discovered Bruce Lee and Chuck Norris. Something immediately connected inside me.

Before karate I felt weak. I was weak.

Different. Socially behind
Bullied constantly.

But martial arts looked like confidence.
Control. Strength. Discipline. Purpose.

Everything I felt like I did not have.

I wanted to train immediately.

The problem was we did not have the resources, and my father absolutely did not approve of martial arts.
So I did what I would continue doing most of my life.

I started trying to figure it out myself.

I remember telling one of my friends that I wanted to become a ninja assassin someday while he told me he wanted to make movies.

Strangely enough, years later we both kind of ended up doing exactly what we said we wanted to do. Well not the Ninja assassin part but definitely the martial arts.

Even before I officially started martial arts, my mind was already consumed with it.

I started reading everything I could get my hands on involving martial arts, ninjas, fighting, discipline, warriors.

Anything.

At the same time I was still trying to figure out basic confidence in life itself.

I couldn't even ride a bike properly yet.

So I secretly taught myself by practicing alone.

One memory from that time stands out vividly.

I saw a bear and moose fighting on their hind legs.

That was just Alaska.

Normal life looked different there.

The Bike Bear

We had moved into our new house on top of a hill about four miles outside of Soldotna, Alaska.

In the prior month I had practiced riding my bike with my brothers some outside with Mom and Dad.

This was one of the few times I remember both of my parents being out side and we were just a family.

My brothers were going off jumps, showing off to Dad. I tried the jump and landed on the bar. Well that ended my riding for that day and week.

At first I had a bad wreck trying to jump the bike and slammed myself right on the middle bar between my legs.

I waited a couple of weeks and thought that I should just get used to riding down the hill we lived on but the road down the hill felt huge to me as a kid.

Probably five hundred to seven hundred feet long and curved hard halfway down.

That will teach you something real quick.

Only two weeks later I had an even bigger wreck.

I tumbled on a dirt gravel road. No helmet. Ouch!

I crashed hard and tumbled across the gravel.

Back then you learned quickly what not to do because pain was usually the teacher.

Two weeks later, after practicing over and over in the yard, I finally worked up the courage to try going down the hill one more time.

I started heading down on more time.
I went past where I had wrecked before. Yay!

I passed the neighbor's house on the left and even waved. "Hey Brittons"

I was feeling pretty good about myself.

Then I stopped looking left and looked ahead.

About three hundred feet away I froze. My mouth went wide open.

There was a brown bear and a moose fighting each other standing on their hind legs right in the middle of the road at the bottom of the hill.

I instantly knew I had to stop.

I slammed on the brakes as hard as I could.

The sound of that back tire scraping across the dirt was unbelievably loud.

Loud enough that both the bear and the moose stopped fighting and turned and looked directly at me.

I remember thinking:

This is it. This is how I die.

About ten or fifteen seconds later my brother came riding down the hill behind me.

He saw what was happening immediately.

He grabbed me by the back of my shirt, jerked me onto the handlebars of his bike, and yelled for me to hold on.

I did.

He pedaled as hard as he could trying to get us back up the hill.
We made it home.

Later we rode back down and looked at the tracks.

The crazy part was after that, for the next three and a half years, I still had to walk through that same bear-infested area every day.

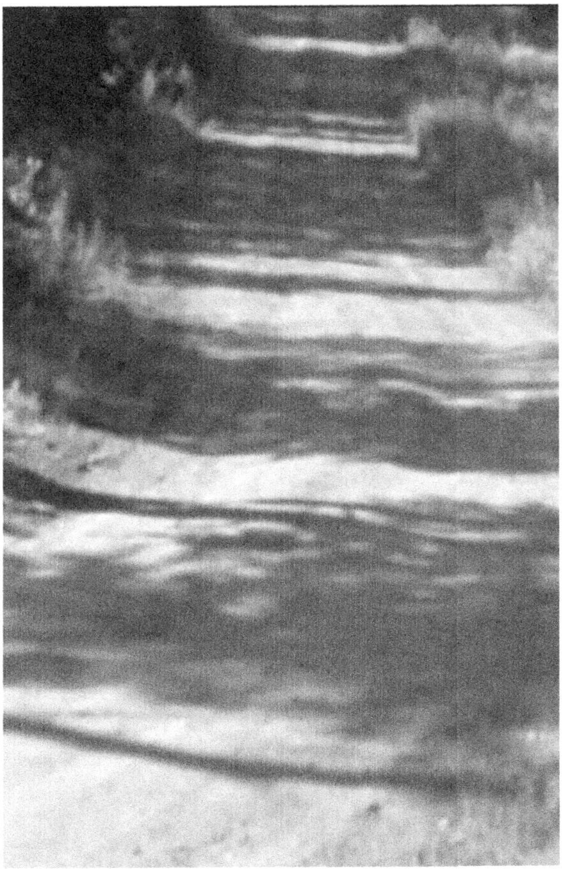

The Lake Bear

Some childhood memories stay sharp because they happen in an instant. The lake was one of those days.

I was out on the water on a small Styrofoam raft with some of the neighborhood kids. It was the kind of thing kids do when there's water nearby.

Floating.
Pushing the raft around.
Enjoying summer.

At that age, the world still feels simple.

Water.
Friends.
Sunlight.

Nothing about the moment felt dangerous.

What I didn't realize was that my brother had been looking for me.

Eventually he found us.

And the moment he saw where we were, everything changed.

He pointed and shouted one word.
"BEAR!"

The word cut through the air instantly.

That was all it took.

The calm lake, the floating raft, the quiet afternoon…

Gone.

My brother had spotted a bear nearby.

Walker Street

When you grow up in Alaska, that word carries a different meaning.

You move.

I got off that raft as fast as I could.

But running straight away from a bear isn't always the smartest move.

Instinct and awareness mix together in those moments.

So I moved until I was out of the bear's sight.

Then I ran.

Fast.

Toward the houses. Toward the neighbors. Toward safety.
Every step felt urgent.

Fear has a way of moving your body before your thoughts catch up.

Run.

That's exactly what I did.

Did I look back?

Yes.

Several times.

But I never stopped until I made it safely home.

By the time I reached the house the adrenaline was still running through me.

The lake that had seemed peaceful only minutes earlier suddenly felt completely different.

Growing up in Alaska teaches you things early.

Nature doesn't always warn you slowly.
Sometimes the warning is one word shouted across the water.

Bear.

And everything changes.

The Walk

From the time I was about eight years old until I was eleven, I walked nearly a mile to and from the bus stop.

In many places that might sound like a simple childhood routine.
In Alaska, it carried a different kind of awareness.
Wildlife was always part of the environment.

On most afternoons I walked home with a neighbor, and I developed a quiet strategy without ever formally discussing it.

I walked fifty to a hundred feet behind her.

At the time it seemed like a small thing.
But the reason was simple.

If something appeared, especially a bear, I would not be the first person it encountered.

It sounds almost strange to say that out loud now, but when you grow up in Alaska those kinds of calculations become normal.

You think about the environment differently. You pay attention.
You stay aware. And you keep moving.

The walk itself was not easy either.
The bus stop was nearly a mile away.
Then another mile coming home.

Winter. Snow. Darkness. Cold.
Repeat. Day after day.

Those walks taught me something that would show up again and again later in life.

Sometimes survival is not about being fearless.

Sometimes it is about understanding the situation you are in and making the smartest move you can.

Walker St

Walking Through Fear

Around age eight one of my friends took me to watch a martial arts class.
I was completely locked in.
I watched everything.

The movements. The discipline. The uniforms. The structure. The confidence. I wanted to be part of it badly.

But since I still did not really have access to training the way other kids did, I took it upon myself to learn however I could.
Books became my instructors before instructors became my instructors.
Any martial arts book I could get my hands on, I studied it.

I would look at the pictures over and over trying to understand movement, stances, techniques, discipline, philosophy.

All of it.

At the same time, I was still making those long walks to and from the bus stop in Alaska.

By then, fear had already become a familiar companion.

Years of isolation, darkness, and constantly paying attention to my surroundings had taught me something before martial arts ever officially did.

You either adapt mentally or you do not.

I think those years built something inside me long before I ever stepped onto a dojo floor.

Fear eventually starts becoming normal when you are exposed to it long enough.

I think that is part of what happened to me during those years.

The Corridor

One of the moments that shaped how I eventually approached teaching martial arts happened long before I ever opened my own dojo.

Her name was Samantha.

She was nine years old and had Down syndrome.

Like many kids her age, she wanted to participate.
To belong.
To feel accepted by the people around her.

But instead of being treated with kindness, she was being bullied.

Watching that situation unfold affected me more deeply than I expected.

At that point in my life, martial arts was still mostly about training, discipline, and personal growth.

I was focused on improving techniques, understanding the art, and becoming better as a practitioner.

But seeing Samantha being mistreated forced me to think about something different.

Protection.

Martial arts had always been described as a way to defend yourself.

But in that moment I began realizing that the deeper purpose of martial arts might be something more than individual self-defense.

It might also be about protecting people who could not easily defend themselves.

Samantha did not need another person telling her she was different.

She already knew the world sometimes treated her differently.

What she needed was someone willing to stand up for her.

That moment stayed with me.

Years later, when I began teaching my own students, I often thought back to situations like that.

Martial arts could build strong athletes.

But it could also build strong character.

It could teach students to stand up for themselves.
And sometimes, just as importantly, it could teach them to stand up for others.

At the time I was already being bullied heavily myself.

Internally I already knew what humiliation felt like.
What isolation felt like.

But I also remember feeling powerless in that moment because I was barely surviving socially myself.

Right after that happened, I remember walking down the corridor next to the cafeteria at Soldotna Elementary School.

And I remember having a thought that would stay with me for the rest of my life. Maybe one day I can help someone like her.

I was only around nine years old.

What is strange is around nine years later, I actually did.

At the time though, I had no idea what that thought would eventually become.

Back then it was just a thought from a bullied kid walking down a school hallway.

Welfare / Survival

The bullying never really stopped.

Then around age eleven my parents got divorced.
Everything got worse after that.
The stability that was already hanging on by a thread, completely collapsed.
We lost our home.

Almost immediately, my 3rd oldest brother and I ended up on public assistance. Welfare from around age eleven until I was eighteen years old.

A lot of people hear the word welfare and instantly form opinions.

But when you are a kid living through it, you are not thinking politically.
You are thinking about survival.

My father eventually abandoned us.

I was the youngest by a good measure, so I watched a lot of this happen while also trying to process everything emotionally at the same time.

The bullying at school was already damaging enough psychologically.
Then home stopped feeling stable too.
There is a certain feeling that comes with suddenly realizing your family is struggling financially and socially at the same time.

You become hyper aware of everything.
What you wear.
What you do not have.
How people look at you.
How other kids live.

What embarrassment feels like.

A lot of people during those years probably had no idea how close internally I was getting to breaking.

But I kept going.
I do not even think I fully understood why at the time.

The Hidden Dangers in Plain Sight

Not long after my parents divorced, my mom wanted to do something good for us.

Life had become survival almost overnight.

We were selling things from the house to help make rent and pay bills. The stability we once had was disappearing piece by piece. Looking back now, I think some of the money came from selling things and some may have come from the divorce itself. I was only eleven, so I didn't fully understand all of it.

What I did understand was this:

We were going to Florida. My mom gave us a choice.
Disney World. Or water parks.
We chose the water parks.
Water Mania.
Wet 'n Wild.

At eleven years old that felt like the right decision.

Part of the trip was also reconnecting with family I barely knew. We visited my cousins, people I had almost no memories with since most of my life had been spent in Alaska.

One afternoon we were outside playing basketball in the driveway.

Alaska kids do things differently.
We throw dirt clods.
Build dirt piles.
Sit on them.
Play in them.

So when I saw a dirt mound nearby, I did the most normal thing in my mind. I sat down. After about 30 seconds.
Instantly it felt like fire. I jumped up screaming.

Fire ants.

I had accidentally sat directly on a fire ant mound.
My cousin looked at me and yelled,

"You sat on the fire ant farm?"

I didn't even know what that was.
"Come on!"

We took off running.

His backyard had a pool, and in my mind the answer was obvious.
Water.

I dove straight in.

Instant relief.

The ants were gone.

Then suddenly I felt him grabbing my shirt.

"Get out! Water moccasin!"

What?

I scrambled out of that pool as fast as I could.
We ran up the ramp toward the glassed in deck area and looked back.
The snake was following us.

We slammed the door shut just as it reached the glass.

Then it struck.

Both of us stood there breathing hard.

Me soaking wet.

Him partly wet because of me.

And all I could think was:

I had just escaped one danger and run straight into another.

That trip meant more to me than I realized.

Life had changed.
My family had changed.

Everything felt uncertain.

But there was also hope.

Water parks.
Family.
New experiences.
Hope.

Even in difficult seasons, life still had moments waiting for us.

Strangely enough, I never lost that love for water parks.

Years later I would still visit them during national championships and travel.

Maybe part of me was always chasing that feeling again.

The feeling that life could still be fun.

Even after everything changed.

Sterling

When my father left, our lives changed almost overnight.
Up until that point we had lived with a certain level of stability.

Not luxury. But enough to feel normal.

When he was gone, that stability disappeared.
We lost almost everything.

At that age you do not fully understand all the financial details, but you understand enough to feel the difference between what your life used to be and what it has become.

It was a difficult time for our family.

Not long after my father left, my mother met another man.
I was around twelve and a half years old when that happened.
Eventually we moved out of town to Sterling, Alaska.
A smaller area outside of Soldotna.

Life there felt very different.

Winter in Alaska is already demanding, but living in Sterling meant we had to rely heavily on wood for heat.

That meant chopping wood. Stacking it.
And making sure there was enough to get through the long cold months.
For a kid that age, it was a lot.

School was not easy either.
In junior high, I was the third smallest boy in the entire school.

That alone can make those years difficult.

But combined with everything else going on in life, it made that period even harder.

There were days when the weight of everything felt overwhelming.

During that time, I felt trapped.

It is not something people like to talk about openly.

But it was part of my reality.

When you feel trapped in an environment where everything seems heavy and uncertain, it can feel like there is no way forward.

Three nights before we left for Anchorage, I remember looking up into the starry Alaska sky and asking God for something very simple.

"God, please get me out of here."

I did not know how it would happen.
I did not know what the future looked like.
I just knew that I needed something to change.

Three days later, something did.

The man my mother had been dating had made it clear that he was never going to marry her.

That realization forced a decision that none of us had expected so quickly.

We packed up and left.
Just like that.

We moved to Anchorage.

Thinking now about that time, that moment feels almost surreal.
Three days after asking for a way out, life changed direction completely.

At the time I could not see the full meaning of it.
I was just a kid trying to survive a difficult chapter of life.

But sometimes the moments that feel like escape are actually the moments where a new path quietly begins.

For me, Anchorage became one of those turning points.

Sterling Martial Arts

Not everything during those years was difficult.

Around that time I finally began training martial arts more consistently. Sterling Elementary offered Tang Soo Do, and for the first time martial arts became a regular part of my life instead of something occasional.

The classes were held in a gym.

Floors. Uniforms. Structure.

Usually twenty to thirty students.
Nobody fooled around much.

People trained seriously.
I loved it.
My 1st instructor was Jeff Warton.

I began riding my bicycle to class because I wanted to train whenever I could. Even during winter.

One day there was already snow on the ground.

Most people probably would have stayed home.

I went anyway.
I took a different route heading there.
More back roads.
More difficult terrain.

So coming home I decided to take the highway.

That decision almost changed everything.

I was riding beside the road on snow and ice.

You cannot hit the brakes hard in those conditions.

If you do, you fall.

In the distance, I saw a semi.

Ahead of me there was a break in the road.

An opening.

If I could reach it, I would be okay.

If not, I would have to ditch the bike into the snow.

I pedaled as hard as I could.

Faster. Faster.

The semi kept coming.

I reached the opening just as it arrived.
I turned.

The bike slid.

I went down.

The semi passed beside me.

Close.

Very close.

Too close.

I lay there in the snow for a moment.

Then got up.

Went home.

That period taught me something important.

Martial arts was already changing me.

Because despite the cold…

Despite the distance…
Despite the danger…

I still wanted to train.

Wrestling

Around that same period, I also wrestled in junior high.

Most people do not know that.

At the time I was still going by Bucky.

I was small.

In fact, during junior high I was one of the smallest students in school.

Wrestling was not easy for me physically.

But it gave me something important.

Pressure. Contact. Being uncomfortable.

And sometimes being the person everybody practiced on.

That mattered more than I realized.

The move to Anchorage would open doors I couldn't yet see, including new oppportunities in martial arts.

Wrestling had already started teaching me how to fall.

I didn't know it at the time, but that wouldn't be the last time someone picked me up and slammed me to the ground.

It happened again in junior high.

Then years later.

Then again in the Army.

Strangely enough, every one of them was a wrestler.

Anchorage

My oldest brother lived in Anchorage, the biggest city in Alaska.

Compared to Soldotna, it felt like another world.

My mom had taken a job as a cocktail waitress at a country western bar in Muldoon in the early 1990s.

Before long she met the man who would become my stepfather, and by the time I was fifteen they were married.

Anchorage accelerated everything.

At school in Soldotna Junior High, I had been a journalist for the school newspaper.
I knew how to use early computer layout programs and design pages for print.

In many subjects I was already a year ahead academically.

When we first arrived in Anchorage I finished the third quarter of eighth grade at Hanshew Middle School.

I liked that school. I was listened to and respected right from the start.
In gym we had to run two one-mile runs over several weeks.
I did not see the point in stretching it out.

I ran both miles two days apart even though they would not let me run them back to back.

But stability was hard to find.
I only stayed with my brother for a short time.
We had to keep moving until we found housing that worked.

Eventually I transferred again.

That final junior high school was Wendler.

And that is where I met someone who would become one of the most important people in my life at the time and am deeply grateful.

Keith P. Sandoval.

Starting Over

At first ,we stayed with my brother for about a month or so while everything was being figured out.

When I enrolled into a new junior high.
I knew absolutely no one. But something changed almost immediately.

For the first time in years I introduced myself as Corey instead of Bucky.
That alone felt like a reset.

I remember saying to my mom, "Let see them rhyme Corey."
Then on my very first day at the largest junior high in Alaska, I was made managing editor.

My first day.

At my previous school I had "only" been a reporter.

Suddenly, I went from being heavily bullied and psychologically beaten down to immediately being given responsibility and recognition.

My confidence shot through the roof.

That experience taught me something I would never forget.
Environment matters.

The right environment can completely change a human being.
I often wonder what would have happened if I had stayed where I was before.

Once I made it to Anchorage, people started seeing me differently.

Eventually, I started seeing myself differently too.

Anchorage Martial Arts

When we moved to Anchorage, martial arts changed again.
In Sterling I had finally found consistency.

Anchorage brought exploration.
For a period of time I trained under Delphin Labrador.

The school exposed me to things I had not experienced before.

Aikido.
Shotokan Karate.
Iaido.

I became his uke often.

Uke - The person being thrown. To receive.

Over. And over. And over again.

Interestingly, I did not realize how valuable that would become.
But learning how to fall is important.

Sometimes on the mat.
Sometimes in life.

Around the same period I also wrestled.

Most people do not know that.

When I left Soldotna and Sterling I ditched the name Bucky forever and started going by my first name Corey.
I was small and grew literally in highschool and not until I left that environment.

One of the smallest kids around.

In wrestling, as I said, I often became the person everyone practiced on.

Wrestling and Aikido were teaching similar lessons.

Pressure. Movement. Impact.
Getting back up.
Eventually we moved again.
That happened a lot.

Between eleven and eighteen, I roughly moved twenty to twenty-five times.

Stability was difficult.

So proximity mattered.
One day I was walking through the mall area and saw a martial arts school opening nearby.

It was close enough to walk to.

That mattered.

I became one of the first students.

My mother enrolled me in the black belt program.

The instructor changed later, and eventually I trained under Bobby Carter.
He was young.

Only around nineteen.
But he could move.

He taught me stretching methods I still remember.

His kicking speed was unbelievable.
Faster than many people could punch.

He came to my dojo one day and he was so happy with my success in Soldotna. This was right about the time I had just renovated the new space. I new he won the Kazuki Challenge and years later I would see footage of him winning the Kazuki Challenge. One of them is still on YouTube.

Around that same period I was also training beside athletes who would later become known names.
Including Sam Hoger.

The Alaskan Assassin.
He fought in UFC 1

At the time none of us knew where life would go.

We were just training.

Anchorage gave me a wide range of martial arrs.

Different instructors.
Different systems.
Different perspectives.

Range

And eventually…

It gave me the path to my first tournament.

THE BUS RIDE TO MY FIRST TOURNAMENT

My first karate tournament came when I was fifteen.
I had been training for only about six months when my former instructor hosted a tournament.

It would be the first time I ever stepped onto a competition floor.

There was one problem. Getting there.

Transportation was not easy for me at the time, but I was not going to miss the opportunity. I figured out the city bus routes and rode across Anchorage to get to the tournament.

Most competitors arrived with their parents.

I arrived by city bus.

But I had been preparing for days.

Even at fifteen, I understood that competition started before you stepped onto the floor.

I made sure I ate well in the days leading up to the tournament.
I drank plenty of water so my mind would be clear and my body ready.

That morning I made sure I ate a good breakfast.
Still, sitting on that bus ride across the city, I was nervous.

And a little hungry.

THE FIRST MATCH

The first time you step onto a tournament floor, the nerves are real.

Your heart is racing.
Your mind is trying to remember everything you have practiced.
But once the match begins, something interesting happens.

The nerves disappear.

You start thinking about what it will take to win.

My first opponent was about 5'11".
Much taller than me.

I stood about 5'7½", so standing in front of him trading punches was not going to work.

Instead, I used movement.

Every time he advanced, I attacked with kicks and forced him to adjust his position.

Little by little he started drifting toward the edge of the ring.
Then the referee stopped the match.

Jogai.

He had stepped out.

We started again.

Another exchange.
Another adjustment.
Again he stepped outside the boundary.
Jogai.

The penalties started adding up.

By the fourth time, the outcome was inevitable.

He had accumulated too many jogai penalties.

The referee disqualified him.

Just like that, I was moving on to the final.

THE FINAL MATCH

The second fight was completely different.

This opponent was even taller.

Around 6'1" or maybe 6'2".

I was still the smaller fighter at 5'7½", and he used his reach well.

The match went back and forth.

In that tournament we were using a half-point, full-point system, and the first fighter to reach three points would win.

Neither of us could pull away.

Points traded.
Momentum shifted.

As the match wound down, the score stood at:
Him: 2.5
Me: 2.0

Only about ten seconds remained.

He launched a right roundhouse kick toward my head.
Instinct took over.

I ducked underneath the kick.

Popped back up.

And drove a reverse punch straight into his chest.

"Yame!" (Stop)
The judges' flags went up.

Point.
The match was over.

For a moment I just stood there.
Then it hit me.

I had won.

My first karate tournament.

Elation.

Release.

After six months of training, I had finally earned a real fighting victory.

The Gold Star

When my freshman year started, I began at East High School, just a brand-new cadet.

After the first quarter, I transferred to Bartlett.
That's where I saw a cadet wearing a gold star.

I asked, "What's that for?"

He said:

"Because we're the best."

That stuck with me.

It reminded me of the line from Men in Black:

"The best of the best."

After that quarter at Bartlett, I returned to East.

I pushed to join the yearbook staff.
At first they refused.
No freshman had ever been allowed before.

But because I had already proven myself doing layout work at Bartlett, they finally let me on as index editor.

Then that summer I went to JROTC camp.

Only four days.

But a lot happened in those four days.

When I returned for my sophomore year,
I came back as a Cadet Second Lieutenant.

The rise had begun.

Henry Babcock

The summer camp after my freshman year changed a lot for me.

It was only four days long, but somehow I came back different. I went in as another cadet and came out with more confidence, more respect, and a promotion waiting for me.

One of the people who noticed was Battalion Commander, Henry Babcock.

Henry was the guy everyone knew. Confident, respected, and the kind of leader people naturally followed. Later on, Keith and I would both chase the same position Henry held, but back then I was just trying to learn.

After camp, Henry kind of took me under his wing.

That mattered more than I realized at the time.

He taught by example. How to carry yourself. How to lead. And occasionally… how to campaign.

Henry ended up becoming king of the Military Ball. There was a vote, and somehow he came up with one of the funniest strategies I had ever seen.

He handed out Oh Henry! candy bars.

Vote for Henry. Get an Oh Henry.
Simple. Clever. Effective.

And it worked.
He won.

To this day I still have the photo. The only one. Henry standing there as Military Ball King.

Looking back, it still makes me laugh.

Military leadership, discipline, competitions… and winning an election with candy bars.

It was brilliant.
But more than that, Henry believed in me. And sometimes when somebody at the top believes in you, you start believing in yourself too.

Not long after that, the rise through the ranks really began.

The Rise Through The Ranks

When my sophomore year began, I returned not as an enlisted cadet.
I returned as an officer.

The four-day summer camp had changed everything.
I had gone in as a freshman still trying to find my place.
I came out a Cadet Second Lieutenant.

From there, the promotions kept coming.

Second Lieutenant. I was in charge of a platoon. I had to show my leadership capabilities and go in front of a promotion board to be promoted.

First Lieutenant. Once made then I would finish out my Sophomore year.
Being promoted over the summer after the camp
then I made Captain during my junior year. I was in charge of one of the companies in the Battalion and Keith was the other commander.

By then, Keith Sandoval and I were no longer just friends.

We were competitors. Rivals.
Both of us pushing toward the same goal.
Battalion Commander.

We each commanded our own companies within the battalion.
And we did everything.

Color Guard. Drill Team. Rifle Team. Honor Guard. Rangers.

We trained together.
Competed together.

Pushed each other constantly.

But the thing I remember most was not the awards.
It was the leadership.

The leaders above us understood something I would carry for the rest of my life:
Real leaders show you the path.

If you listen, they show you everything.
A lot of people probably thought I was headed toward the military.

For a while, I thought so too.

But martial arts never really left.
It stayed in the background the entire time.

The movies, philosophy. and discipline,
The desire to become stronger mentally and physically.
The difference now was I was not the same kid who arrived in Anchorage.
The bullying years had not disappeared.

But confidence had started replacing fear.
Environment, leadership and responsibility all matter.

And somewhere underneath all of it...
the same spark from The Karate Kid was still there.

Waiting.

Battalion Commander

The funny thing is, that gold star was never really supposed to be mine.
I only wore it at Bartlett for one quarter before transferring back to East, but I never forgot it.

I still remember asking why they wore it and being told, "Because we're the best."
Simple answer.
But it stuck.

At the same time I was bouncing between schools and trying to figure out where I fit. Bartlett gave me a chance to prove myself doing layout and when I transferred back to East, that finally opened the door for me there too. That's when i completed yearbook index for the yearbook in about 2 weeks.

Meanwhile JROTC was moving fast.

Summer camp after my freshman year changed everything. I went in as a private and came out a second lieutenant. After that Henry Babcock took me under his wing. This was the same Henry who somehow became king of the military ball by handing out Oh Henry candy bars and getting everyone to vote for him. Still one of the smartest campaign ideas I ever saw.
The years moved quickly after that. Keith and I kept pushing through Drill Team, Color Guard, Rifle Team, Honor Guard, Rangers, and leadership positions. Along the way I earned Superior Cadet my sophomore, junior, and senior years. Only one male and one female received that award at each grade level.

I was also selected for Cadet of the Year twice. Out of roughly a thousand cadets, I finished in the top eight both times.

Second place.
Twice.

At the time that bothered me.

Now, it doesn't.

By the end of my junior year I was announced as Battalion Commander for senior year and served three of the four quarters because it gave us the best chance to win.

I left a legacy there.

WE WON!

RFI.

Regional Formal Inspection. The coveted "GOLD" star. R.F.I. only comes around once every four years and there are seven high schools competing for the top spot and the right to say they are the best for the next four years.

The same gold star I first saw at Bartlett was now ours.
Not because I wore it for a quarter.

Because it was earned by those before me.

To this day, that still feels strange. The kid bouncing between schools my freshman year, trying to get onto yearbook, and staring at someone else's gold star ended up helping lead East High to earn one too.

Funny how life works sometimes.

Martial Arts Becoming Real

Society sees karate as rigid and structured. Strict. Hard. Disciplined.
But what about life? Is life easy? Life is harder than karate.
Karate has rules. Life does not.

In karate, there are boundaries, instructors, time limits, referees, and a clear beginning and end. You bow in. You train. You improve. You bow out. Life does not work that way.

Life throws things at you when you are not ready. It does not care about rank, titles, experience, sacrifice, or effort. It just comes.

The irony is that everything I learned and taught in martial arts eventually became the very thing I needed to survive life itself. The discipline. The perseverance.

The ability to keep moving forward when I was exhausted.
The ability to take one more step when I did not want to.

Martial arts was never just becoming stronger physically. It was preparation for life.

I just did not realize it at the time.

The Checkout Line

Life has a strange way of changing direction in ordinary places. For me, it happened in a checkout line at Sam's Club.

In late 96', early 97'. I was working at Sam's, scanning items and helping customers like I did every day. Nothing about that shift felt different. Then, my old Sensei walked up to my register.

I had not been to class in a while, and the moment I saw him I felt embarrassed. Without thinking, I said, "I'm sorry I haven't been in class, Sensei."

He looked at me calmly and said, "That's okay."

That was it. The transaction ended, and he walked away. At the time it felt like a small, awkward moment. Just a former student running into his instructor at work. But two days later everything changed.

He came through my line again and asked if he could speak with me about an opportunity and to meet him at his school. When I arrived, he offered me a job. Not just a job working in the school, but an opportunity to learn how to teach karate and eventually open a school under his organization.

I walked into Sam's Club that day expecting another ordinary shift behind a register. Instead, two short conversations in a checkout line changed the direction of my life.

It almost feels like the opening scene of a movie.

One register. One apology. One instructor.

And suddenly, the path began.

Figure It Out

One of the first major moments that changed how I viewed teaching happened early while I was learning how to instruct.

My old Sensei pointed at a student named Octavian Mosesian and told me to teach him.

I immediately responded:

"But he is missing an arm and a leg."

My old Sensei looked at me and simply said:
"Figure it out."

That was it.

No long explanation. No instructional manual. No step-by-step process.

Just: Figure. It. Out.
So I did.

Octavian trained alongside his brother Andreas Mosesian, and about four months later both of them earned their yellow belts.

That moment hit me hard mentally.
Because somewhere during that process I started realizing something important.

If these guys could do it, anyone could.
That idea changed everything for me.
Not just about martial arts. About people.

Limits. Confidence. Teaching. Adaptation. Possibility.

I think that was one of the earliest foundational moments behind the philosophy that would later shape Green's Karate and eventually Karate Wise.

I did not know it then, but that moment would eventually become part of the foundation for everything that followed. The students. The methods. The teaching system. The athletes. Even the invention years later.

I just did not understand what I was building yet.

The First Signs

After teaching Octavian Mosesian and Andreas Mosesian, something started changing in how I viewed instruction.

I stopped looking at students as "Can they do karate?" and started looking at: "How do I help THIS person understand?"

That became the puzzle.

Not everybody learned the same. Not everybody moved the same. Not everybody processed information the same. Not everybody had the same confidence level. Not everybody responded to pressure the same way.

Most instructors at the time were teaching one way to everybody.

I started naturally adapting.

Without realizing it yet, I was beginning to study learning itself: body language, confidence, fear, timing, energy, attention span, frustration, and motivation.

Because I had spent years being bullied, isolated, awkward socially, and mentally fighting my own battles growing up, I think I naturally connected with students that struggled differently than other instructors did.

I understood embarrassment. I understood frustration. I understood what it felt like to feel behind.

What I did not realize yet was that all of those earlier painful years were slowly becoming tools.

At the time though, I was just trying to become a better instructor.

Returning to Soldotna

Earlier that year my old Sensei asked me a question.

He asked me if I thought opening a dojo in Soldotna was a good idea.
I told him yes.
I used to live there. Went to elementary school there. Went to middle school there.

What I did not tell him was what those years were actually like for me.

The bullying. The isolation. The humiliation. How much I had hated parts of my childhood there.

I kept all of that to myself.

At the time though, I think something inside me recognized this as an opportunity to go back and make a difference in the same community that had nearly broken me psychologically as a kid.

Not through revenge.

Through helping people.

Helping kids like myself build confidence, self-discipline, self-defense, and direction.

In August of 1997 he awarded me my black belt.

That was also the last time I ever physically saw him.

Before I drove to Soldotna, we had an argument about my pay structure.
I tried negotiating.

He held firm.

The arrangement was that I would receive $1,300 base pay instead of the normal $1,500 the other instructors received.

Then for the first three months, $200 of my $400 commission would be garnished.

If I did not hit $10,000 in revenue, my commission dropped from 4% to 3%.

At the time I accepted the arrangement because I believed in the opportunity and believed this was going to become my long-term career.

So in September of 1997, I moved forward and helped open the school in Soldotna.

At that exact moment, I officially became a Sensei.

I was also the youngest person in the history of their organization to ever open and run one of their schools.

And not just any school.

This was the school furthest away from the main location in Anchorage.

By the end of 1997, everything was starting to come apart.

The situation at the dojo no longer felt stable, and mentally I was trying to figure out what I was supposed to do next.

Part of what bothered me was not the money itself.

It was trust.

The agreement had been simple.

I earned a four percent commission, but half of it was taken during a probation period. I was told that if I generated at least $10,000 a month for three consecutive months, I would receive the full commission.

So I went to work.

By the end of November, the program had generated roughly $34,000. Every month had been over $10,000.

I had done exactly what I was told I needed to do.

Then on December 5th, I was informed the target had changed.

Now the goal was $15,000 for December.

That was the moment something shifted inside me.

The numbers were not really the issue.

The issue was that I had met the original agreement and suddenly the finish line had moved.

That Christmas break became one long mental battle trying to figure out my future.

At the same time I was also trying to become a 911 dispatcher because honestly I thought maybe that would become my next career path.

Something stable.

Reliable.
Predictable.
But that fell through too.

Now I was sitting there trying to figure out how to survive financially with no real backup plan.
The one thing I could not ignore was what the previous three months had already shown me.

I knew how to teach, enroll students, and build a program.
The numbers had proven that.

I started looking at possible locations to open my own dojo.

One gym owner wanted ninety percent commission.

I remember sitting there thinking she was completely out of her mind.
I thanked her for her time and walked out.

Then I found another gym.

Much more reasonable.

The agreement came out to around $718 a month for four days a week and two classes each evening.

For the first time, the idea felt possible.
Not easy.
But possible.

At that point I realized I was down to two choices.

Start over completely.
Or bet on myself.

In January of 1998, I walked into the bank and took out a $1,500 signature loan.

That money had to cover everything.

Rent.

Insurance.

The sign.

Office setup.

Anything I absolutely needed to get the doors open.

It is amazing how little money separated failure from opportunity.

Fifteen hundred dollars.
That was it.

That loan became the foundation of everything that followed.
Green's Karate opened on January 17, 1998.

Second Day

On the second day after opening my dojo, there was a knock at the door. It was the new instructor.

He walked in angry.

At that point word had already spread that I had left and opened my own school.

The conversation escalated quickly.
At one point he called me a "chicken **** bastard" and told me my black belt was revoked.

Then he told me to give him my belt.

I remember looking at him and saying:
"I'm not giving you my belt. No way. I earned it."

He was not happy.

But he said he was not done with me either.

I still remember standing there processing what was happening.
Just days earlier I was trying to figure out how to survive financially and emotionally after walking away from everything I thought was going to be my future.

Now suddenly I was being told my black belt meant nothing anymore.

Looking back now, moments like that either break people mentally or force them to become stronger.

At the time though, it just added even more pressure onto an already terrifying situation.

Because now it really was all on me.

No organization. No protection. No safety net.

Just me trying to build something from scratch while people around me were actively telling me I would fail.

The First Students

Once the doors opened, reality hit fast.

Now it was all on me.

No organization above me. No guaranteed paycheck. No safety net. No fallback plan.

Just me standing inside a small dojo in Soldotna hoping enough people would walk through the doors for this thing to survive.

I did everything myself.
Teaching. Cleaning. Phone calls. Enrollment. Paperwork. Advertising. Talking to parents. Setting up equipment. Breaking everything down afterward.

Everything.

At first every new student mattered massively.
One student felt important. Two students felt important. Five students felt important.

Because every enrollment meant maybe I could survive another month.

I think a lot of people imagine entrepreneurship as freedom.

In the beginning it felt more like pressure. Constant pressure.

If class attendance dropped, I noticed. If somebody quit, I noticed. If money got tight, I noticed.

There was no separation between my life and the dojo.

The dojo was my life.
But something else started happening too.

I started seeing confidence changes in students.

Kids standing taller. More eye contact. Parents noticing changes at home.

Shy students opening up. Bullied kids starting to believe in themselves more.

That started affecting me deeply because I understood exactly what some of those kids were feeling internally.

A lot of them reminded me of myself growing up.

And slowly I started realizing maybe this dojo was becoming something bigger than just a business.

Maybe this was becoming purpose.

two weeks after opening, I made $3,000 in two weeks. I went back to the back and paid back my loan in full immediately.

Once back at the dojo I remember saying to myself.

This is FREEDOM

Little did I know at the time how much my life would later become a fight to protect that freedom.

The Floor Bounced

The first dojo was an old aerobics and exercise floor in Soldotna, Alaska.

The floor bounced when you walked across it. Not a little. Enough to notice.

It was not built for karate. It was built for step classes and workout music.

But it was the only place I could afford.
And to me, it looked like opportunity.

I can still remember standing there looking at the room while everything echoed. Empty walls. Empty floor. Just possibility.

I remember thinking:

This is either going to work… or I'm about to learn a very hard lesson.
Little by little the empty room started looking less like an aerobics floor and more like a dojo.

Not a perfect dojo. But a real one.

And somewhere inside all that uncertainty, something happened that I had never fully experienced before.

Freedom.

For the first time in my life, I was not following someone else's system.

I was building my own.

The Doors Open

The strange thing about opening a dojo is that after all the planning, stress, and worrying… eventually you have to unlock the door and see if anybody actually shows up.

That is the moment where the dream stops being imaginary.

I remember those first days wondering if people would even walk through the door. Soldotna was not exactly overflowing with martial arts schools back then, but that did not guarantee success either. Just because a town does not have something does not mean the town wants it.

At first, every new student felt enormous.

Every phone call mattered.
Every parent walking through the door mattered.
Every class mattered.

I taught like my future depended on it because… it did.

The floor still bounced beneath our feet during training. Every stance, every kick, every movement reminded me this place had once been designed for aerobics instead of karate. But little by little the room started changing identity.

The mirrors reflected students lined up in rows instead of workout classes.

The sound of music was replaced by students counting, kiais echoing across the floor, and the sharp snapping sound of techniques being thrown with purpose.

That room slowly stopped feeling borrowed.

It started feeling like ours.

When i first opened I remember thinking that I was going to show the world what people with special needs can do.

At the time I knew I was changing students.

Helping kids. Building confidence. Giving people tools to make life easier.

Especially some of the students with special needs.

What happened afterward changed the way I thought about that moment.

Because decades later many of those same kinds of students would end up helping me through parts of my own life.

I started by helping them. Later, they helped me.

I just had not lived that part yet.

60 in 6 Months

Momentum is a strange thing.

At first you fight for every inch of it. Every student feels like a victory because you know exactly how much is riding on it.

Then one day you look around and realize something has changed.

The dojo was not empty anymore.

Classes were filling up.

Students lined up across that old bouncing aerobics floor while parents sat watching from the side. The sound inside the room changed too. What had once echoed now carried energy. Kiais. Movement. Conversations before class. Kids laughing. Pads popping. Belt tests approaching.

The place had become alive.

By six months in, I had around sixty students.

Sixty.

That number meant more to me than people probably realized because six months earlier all I had was a $1,500 loan, an empty room, and a vision nobody else could fully see yet.

Now people were trusting me with their kids, their time, their goals, and their money.

That responsibility hit me hard.
Somewhere during that growth I stopped feeling like a guy trying to run a dojo.

I became a dojo owner.

Not pretending.
Not imagining it.
Real.

Up to that point I had built almost everything on instinct.

The school was growing.
Students were coming.
The tournaments were starting.
Parents trusted me.

People thought I had it figured out.

Truth was, I was figuring it out one day at a time.

And somewhere in the middle of all that success, I realized something important.

I still needed a Sensei.

Not because I was failing.

Because I was growing.

Soldotna gave me more than I realized.

20 minutes in Summer. 30 in Winter

Success has a way of making young entrepreneurs feel invincible.
By the time the dojo crossed one hundred students, my mind was already moving ahead of where I was standing. That is both a gift and a dangerous habit.

I started realizing something important. People wanted to learn.

Not just karate either.

Kickboxing was starting to catch attention too. Adults wanted fitness. Teenagers wanted intensity. Parents wanted structure for their kids.

The demand was growing faster than I expected.
Somewhere in the middle of all that momentum, I made another decision that probably sounded crazy to most people around me.

I opened a second location in Nikiski.
Six months after opening my first dojo.

Years later, I realize how aggressive that move really was.
Most people would have stayed comfortable.
Protected what they already built.

Waited.

I did not think that way back then.
All I could see was opportunity.

Nikiski was about twenty minutes away in the summer.

Thirty in the winter.

And in Alaska, those extra ten minutes matter.

The strip mall deal itself was incredible.
The location was around sixteen hundred square feet.
The agreement was simple.
Any non-homeschool student was $10 a month.

If I had twenty homeschool students and twenty non-homeschool students, the rent was only around $200 a month.

That was the deal.

For the first year.

To a young entrepreneur trying to expand, it looked amazing.
Then renewal came.

The increase was one thousand percent.
Suddenly the rent jumped to around $2,000 a month.

That rivaled the rent of my main dojo.

This was also Nikiski, Alaska.

Literally the end of the road.
A dead end.

I had to move the dojo.

The students were changing.

Kids who barely spoke began volunteering answers. Students who struggled to focus started finishing the entire class.

Parents were telling me stories and positive results I never saw inside the dojo.

Shy students opening up. Bullied kids starting to believe in themselves.

That affected me deeply because I understood exactly what some of those kids were feeling internally.

What interested me most wasn't the technique. I realized I was doing more than teaching techniques.

I was studying learning.

How people moved. How they understood. How they got stuck. How they grew.

I did not know it then, but those observations would later become methods, systems, teaching layers, and eventually things far bigger than that.

I just thought I was helping students.

The Techno Collective

Somewhere in the middle of running two martial arts schools, my life took another strange turn.

I got offered a Monday night radio show. For free. Two hours. Nine to eleven at night.

Most people probably would have said no. I was already stretched thin teaching classes, driving between Soldotna and Nikiski, trying to manage growth, answering phones, and figuring out how to run two schools at barely twenty years old.

But something about it sounded exciting. Creative. Different.

So I said yes.

That is how The Techno Collective with DJ Deep Freeze was born.
The station was WPLZ.

On Monday nights, for two hours, I stepped into an entirely different world.

During the day I was "Sensei."

At night I became DJ Deep Freeze.

Headphones on. Microphone live. Techno music pumping through radios across the Kenai Peninsula.

It sounds surreal now looking back on it, but at the time it felt completely normal. My life already moved at such a chaotic pace that adding a radio show somehow made sense.

The funny thing is, the skills were not actually that different.

Teaching karate and controlling the energy of a room has rhythm to it.

DJing has rhythm too.

You read people. You control pacing. You build energy. You understand timing.

A class has flow.
Music has flow.

I did not fully understand it back then, but both worlds required the same thing:

Presence

Matrix Moves

There is a moment when you realize you are not just playing music anymore. You are controlling a room. The energy shifts when you want it to. People move when you tell them to. Relationships start and end on your timing. The right song at the right moment changes everything. That was where I was. Running two dojos by day and DJing six nights a week by night.

That night a girl came up to me. She looked like Demi Moore. She wanted a slow dance. The problem was the next song up was fast. A banger. I told her I would take care of it. I went up to the booth looking for the right track. Then I saw something shiny coming straight at me fast. I adjusted. Head left. Body right. Just enough. A glass ashtray missed its target and found me instead. The razor-thin edge caught me across the bridge of my nose.

I touched my face. Blood. The song was ending. I switched the track, walked back out, and asked her to dance. At first she looked at me strange. Then she saw the blood. While we danced, I explained what had happened and told her I was probably headed to the hospital afterward.

After the dance I went back to the booth, switched songs again, told them someone else needed to take over, and drove myself to the hospital.

Eleven stitches.

I know... it sounds insane.

But I still got the dance.

We ended up dating.

4,000 Square Feet

Growth changes the way you think.

At first all you want is enough students to survive. Enough income to pay the rent. Enough momentum to prove you were not crazy for taking the risk in the first place.

But once growth starts happening consistently, your mind shifts into another mode.

Expansion.

That is where I was headed.

The original aerobics floor had served its purpose, but the school was growing beyond what that space comfortably allowed. Classes were fuller. Energy was higher. More students kept coming through the doors.

So in January of 1999, I made another move.

I expanded into a four-thousand-square-foot dojo directly beneath the aerobics floor.

Four thousand square feet.

At that age, that felt enormous.

My brother came up from the lower forty-eight and helped me build it out. We built the locker room walls ourselves. Piece by piece the place transformed from an empty commercial space into a dojo.
I installed a wall of mirrors.

Blue mats stretched across the floor.

The sound changed too.

Bigger room, echo. and energy.

I can still remember standing there looking across that open floor realizing how far things had come in such a short amount of time.

Just a year earlier I had taken out a $1,500 signature loan with no guarantees and almost no safety net.

Now I was standing inside a four-thousand-square-foot dojo built through momentum, risk, and belief.

At that moment, it felt like the gamble had paid off.

I MADE IT

October of 1998 was an important month for me because I finally found a Sensei again.

Up to that point I had been building mostly on instinct. The school was exploding. Students kept coming in. Parents kept talking. Word spread. We reached around one hundred eighty students in about eleven months, and I was only twenty-one years old.

People asked my age almost every day.
"How old are you?"
"How old do you think I am?" I would ask back.
"Twenty-five? Twenty-six?"
"You're close."

Then they would ask again and I would smile and tell them I did not disclose my age. I did that for almost two straight years because people simply could not believe someone that young had built what I had built.

Some respected it. Some did not. That was one of my first lessons as an entrepreneur.

You cannot make everyone happy.

In December of 1998 I signed the lease on a four-thousand-square-foot facility and moved in during January of 1999. I still remember standing in the middle of that building before it officially became a dojo. Shoes still on. Empty floor. Mirrors. Locker rooms. Benches. Office space.
Just looking around thinking:

Wow… I made it.

One year earlier I had taken out a $1,500 signature loan and opened on a bouncing aerobics floor.

Now I had the biggest martial arts school in the same town where I had been bullied.

That full circle hit me hard.

One day I looked outside and saw one of the guys who had bullied me years earlier walking past. I ran out the door and called his name.

“Remember that fight we got into when we were thirteen?”

He turned around completely shocked.

Then I smiled.

“Thank you. You inspired me to go ALL THE WAY.”

And strangely enough, I meant it.

The bullying. The isolation. The embarrassment. All of it had become fuel. Around that same time we started competing. The first tournament we attended we took third place out of seventeen martial arts schools. The second tournament we took second. Sensei Tanaka had dominated Alaska for years, so realistically second was probably the highest I could have reached.

We reached it anyway.

I know Soldotna gave me more than I thought I could face at the time. The pain. The pressure. The fights. The lessons.

I just didn't understand what it was building.

Every Sunday from October of 1998 forward, I trained with Tanaka-sensei.

Those Sundays mattered.

The standard never changed.

Not then. Not now.

The same standards that existed when I opened Green’s Karate in 1998 still exist today.

Society changed.

The standard did not.

I remember standing in my dojo at twenty-one years old, teaching classes in a building I had built from nothing, I felt pride for the first time.

Not because of trophies.
Not because of money.

Because I had built something real.

Students were learning. Parents were trusting me. The school was growing faster than I ever imagined. For the first time in my life it felt like I had momentum instead of resistance.

I was young.

Confident.
Maybe a little too confident.
Success has a way of doing that.

You start believing the hard part is over.
You start thinking you finally outran the things that chased you.
Looking back now, I realize life was not done teaching me yet.

Not even close.

The dojo was growing.
The tournaments were coming.
My confidence was rising.

And somewhere ahead was another lesson waiting for me.

I just did not know it yet.

The Avalanche Road

January 31st through February 1st of 2000.
That date matters because people can look it up.
At the time, I was taking Angela to Anchorage so she could meet my Sensei. There is only one road from Soldotna to Anchorage. You drive through the mountains around Turnagain Arm, past Alyeska, past Beluga Point, and eventually into Anchorage.
It felt like a normal drive.

No cell phones, no alerts AND...
no idea what was happening behind us.

We finally arrived at my Sensei's dojo and he opened the door abruptly. He looked relieved.

Almost out of breath.

"Oh thank goodness you made it."
I looked at him confused.
"What are you talking about?"
"You cannot go home."
"What do you mean?"
"Avalanches."
I remember repeating it back.
"Avalanches?"

He explained that while we had been driving, avalanche after avalanche had come down behind us along the route.

At that point there were already over a dozen.

The final count ended up being seventeen.
Some were reported to be nearly a mile wide.
Some buried sections around thirty feet deep.

The story was everywhere.

And somehow we had driven through all of it without knowing.

Angela eventually flew home with help from her dad.
I stayed in Anchorage.

For a week.

Toward the end the Red Cross helped me with a hotel because I had not planned for any of this. Even though the dojo was doing well, life still happened. Rent. Bills. Timing. Money already allocated somewhere else.

I had not prepared to be trapped by a mountain.

I think that experience stayed with me because I was literally driving toward my future while danger was quietly unfolding behind me.

That pattern would return in my life more than once.

Success growing while problems formed in the background.

Building while life moved behind me.

Moving forward while danger followed.

At the time, I thought I had simply survived an avalanche.

I did not realize life had just introduced me to one of its recurring lessons.

Things can change without warning.

And they often do.

Photo: Don Bachman

The improbable part is not what happened.

The improbable part is that I lived long enough to tell the story.

The Wrestler

Around that time I was dating Angela. I was twenty-one. She was nineteen, and honestly I thought she might eventually become my wife. Life felt wide open then. The dojos were growing fast, the second location was running, the radio show had started, and I had finally found a Sensei again. It felt like everything was moving in the right direction.

One night, her brother wanted to wrestle. He wass a state champion wrestler. At first, I thought we were just messing around, but it quickly became obvious he was trying to hurt me. I tried walking away. Instead he came up from behind, locked his arms around me in a bear hug, and tried to lift and dump me. Instinct took over. I dropped into Sanchin dachi and sank my weight. He could not move me.

I told him calmly, "Let me go." He did not. So I warned him. "I'll count to three. If you don't let go, I'm going to break something." I counted. One. Two. Three. He still did not let go. So I broke his wrist. Then, hoping he would not realize it immediately, I put it back into place. Three days later I saw him at a restaurant wearing a cast.

Oddly enough, after that we became friends. Life has a strange way of doing that sometimes.

What a Kick

By early 2000, life was moving fast.

The dojos were growing. Students kept coming in. I was teaching, driving between locations, running programs, DJing on the radio, working clubs at night, and trying to keep up with all of it at the same time.
Somewhere in the middle of all that, a newspaper article came out.

"What a Kick."

It was strange seeing my story in print because I still saw myself as the kid that had struggled growing up. The bullying. The isolation. The lack of confidence. Now there was a newspaper talking about the schools and what was happening in the community.

The article focused on the growth of the dojo and martial arts in Soldotna. Students were coming in. Classes were filling. Parents were talking. The school had momentum.

What people did not see was everything happening behind the scenes.

Running two locations. Teaching classes. Driving constantly. Radio. Clubs.

Building programs. Trying to stay ahead of growth while figuring everything out in real time.

From the outside, life probably looked exciting.

Young dojo owner.

Two schools.
Radio.
DJ.
Newspaper articles.

Everything moving forward.

What nobody saw was how fast life was moving underneath all of it.

"What a Kick," became one of the first public signs that Green's Karate was becoming something real.

The schools were growing.
Momentum was building.

Life looked like it was moving in the right direction.

Just weeks earlier I had unknowingly driven through avalanche country and missed disaster by minutes.

I thought that was the close call.

I was wrong.

The mountain had already tested me.

Now life was about to.

PENINSULA LIFE

What a kick!

Karate class challenges spirit, mind, body of disabled students

Story by Sara J. Smith
Photos by M. Scott Moon

People aren't only ones affected by winter blahs

...Karate

The Discovery

Two weeks after the avalanche incident, life changed again.

At the time, I thought I was in love.

A week earlier we had driven together to Anchorage so I could train with my Sensei. We had unknowingly passed through the mountains minutes before seventeen avalanches came down behind us.

At the time, it felt like we had escaped something.

I had no idea another avalanche was coming.

One night we were at Sal's in Soldotna, a legendary twenty-four-hour restaurant known for its French toast. Behind it was a dance club.
I wanted to go dancing.

Angela could not get in because she was nineteen and the age limit was twenty-one.

She kissed me goodbye and said she was going to spend time with friends at a nearby house.

That kiss turned out to be the last one.

The next morning, on the way to train with Sensei, I decided to stop by the house just to say hello.

A guy answered the door.

"Angela here?" I asked.

"Yeah," he said. "Second door on the right."

I walked down the hallway.
Opened the door.
She was in bed with another man.
I pulled the covers back just enough to know the truth.
Then I left.

No yelling.
No fight.
No scene.

Just silence.

That morning I still drove to Anchorage and trained again.

I think martial arts became the place I went when life hurt.

Just weeks earlier I had unknowingly driven through avalanche country and missed disaster by minutes.

I thought that was the close call.

I was wrong.

Avalanches do not always come from mountains.

Sometimes they come from people.

The Dojo Continued...

Life did not stop after that.

The dojos were still there. Students still showed up. Parents still had questions. Classes still had to be taught.

At the time I was running Soldotna and Nikiski, teaching classes, driving back and forth, DJing on the radio, working clubs, and trying to keep up with growth while life kept moving around me.

I think the dojo became the place where I re-centered.

No matter what happened personally, students still needed me. Parents still trusted me. Kids were still changing. Confidence was still growing.

The strange thing was that while everything felt chaotic personally, the outside world kept moving forward.

The schools were growing.
The newspaper article had come out.
Momentum was building.

And without realizing it yet, another opportunity was already on its way.

Alaska Men

A week after everything happened with Angela, my mom brought something up again.

It was not the first time either. She had probably mentioned it five times over the previous few years.

"You should call Alaska Men Magazine."

This time I finally listened.

I drove three hours to meet the owner, Susie Smutz. We met at a Wendy's. I showed up wearing gray sweats and a T-shirt with my hair sticking up everywhere like a troll doll. I did not care what I looked like. At that point I was running dojos, teaching classes, DJing on the radio, working clubs, and trying to keep up with life.

She started asking questions about everything. The schools. Radio. DJ work. The clubs. Growth. Then she told me she wanted to come down and photograph it.

A few days later she arrived in a motorhome and started taking pictures everywhere. The dojo. The radio station. The club. Guys were even lining up hoping to be part of the magazine. Toward the end we ran out of volunteers, so my friend Kalani and I started taking pictures behind the dojo. One on a small cabin. One on a rock. Looking back now it was basically an accidental GQ photoshoot behind a martial arts school in Alaska.

I had absolutely no idea those pictures were about to change my life.

Three weeks later the phone rang.

It was Susie.

"All your wildest dreams are about to come true."

I laughed.

"What are you talking about?"

She told me a magazine was about to call.

"They want you to represent Alaska."

"Who?"

She paused.

"Cosmopolitan."

I still laugh at my response.

"I've never heard of them."

The Call

A few weeks after the photoshoot, the phone rang.
It was Cosmopolitan.
They asked a simple question.

"Do we need to send a photographer to Alaska, or would you like to travel?"

Then they gave me three choices.

California.
Miami.
New York.

I had already gone to California for my twenty-first birthday not long before that. I stayed with my stepdad's daughter and her husband, who happened to be an F-18 fighter pilot. She worked at the officers' club on base.

My twenty-first birthday had been spent around F-18 fighter pilots at an officers' club in California.

Looking back now, it sounds like something out of a movie.

At the time, it was just life.

California already felt familiar.

So I picked it.

Looking back now, it is funny how normal all of this felt while it was happening.

I was still the same guy running dojos in Alaska, teaching classes, DJing on the radio, working clubs at night, and trying to keep everything moving.

Nothing about my life felt glamorous.

Then suddenly Cosmopolitan was calling.

The strange thing was I still did not fully understand what was happening.

I had never even heard of the magazine.

To me it was just another opportunity.
Another adventure.

I had no idea I was about to end up in Los Angeles, standing in a mansion with professional models while wearing a suit that cost more than I probably had in my bank account.

Life was getting strange again.

Sunset Strip

I landed in California, rented a Dodge Dakota pickup, and started exploring.

I went to the Laugh Factory and ended up hanging around comedians afterward. They invited me to join them at Pink's Hot Dogs, which at the time felt like one of the strangest food experiences I had ever had. I obliged.

Later that night, I ended up at a bar on the Sunset Strip and started talking with a guy sitting nearby.

I asked him what he did.

He told me he was a martial artist who trained celebrities.

I asked him what he charged?

He said $500.00/hr. in 2000.

Even back then I remember thinking:

What kind of life is this?

At one point I also visited a Taekwondo school that had an actual creek running through the middle of the dojang. Years later I would see that same place on television during a show about plastic surgeons and realize I had trained there for a day.

I was just exploring.

Seeing the world.

Later that night I went to a club.

I paid what they called a "C-note" to get in.

One hundred dollars.

The guy at the door nodded and let me through the velvet rope.

Inside, I immediately realized I was somewhere very different from Soldotna, Alaska.

Celebrities were everywhere.

One of the first people I saw was Christopher "Play" Martin from House

Party. He was surrounded by about seven women.

I looked around for a moment and thought:

I do not think I belong here.

So I left.

I had a Cosmopolitan photoshoot the next morning.

The Mansion

The next day, I was told to arrive at a hotel where three white vans would pick us up and take us to the location.

I arrived early and waited.

Ten o'clock came and went.

At 10:05 a white motorhome pulled into the parking lot. I walked up and knocked on the window.

A woman opened it.

"Excuse me," I asked. "Are you with Cosmopolitan magazine?"

With complete confidence she replied:

"Ah Nah honey, we're with Macy's."

I laughed.

"Never heard of you."

A few minutes later the three white vans finally arrived. About a dozen of us piled in and headed into the hills near the Hollywood sign.

We pulled up to a mansion worth around three million dollars.
Inside were photographers, stylists, makeup artists, wardrobe people, and the Cosmopolitan crew. Most of the other guys were professional models. I was just a martial arts instructor from Alaska who somehow ended up there.

They did hair, makeup, wardrobe.

The whole thing felt unreal.

When they handed me a suit I asked two questions.

"What kind of suit is it?"

"How much?"

"Dolce & Gabbana."

About two thousand dollars.

I was holding a Coke when they told me that.
I immediately set it down and grabbed water.
I was not spilling anything on a two-thousand-dollar suit.

In the entire shoot, I ended up being the only guy wearing a full suit and tie.
Later, they had us standing shirtless on a winding staircase for another photo.

The only problem was I had absolutely no tan.

After the shoot I still had time before heading back, so I kept exploring.
California still felt unreal to me.

A martial arts instructor from Alaska hanging around comedians, driving the Sunset Strip, meeting celebrity trainers, standing in mansions in Hollywood, and somehow ending up in Cosmopolitan magazine.

I remember thinking:

What kind of life is this?

After I got home another package arrived.

It was from *Cosmopolitan.*

Inside were toiletries, cologne, other items, and a letter. The photoshoot was already over, but somehow the whole thing still felt like it was moving.

We already knew New York was coming.

The launch trip.
The events.
The magazine rollout.

About six weeks later, I would be flying across the country again. Not for karate. Not for competition. Not for the military.

For Cosmopolitan.

I had already stood in a mansion in Hollywood wearing a two-thousand-dollar suit. Now New York was next.

The whole thing was ridiculous.

And I was enjoying every minute of it.

New York

Six weeks later, I landed in New Jersey and took my first yellow cab into Manhattan.

Within minutes I realized those cab drivers might be some of the best drivers in the world. They were weaving through traffic within inches of other cars like it was completely normal. I just sat there thinking, these people can drive.

When I arrived at the hotel, Cosmopolitan had already taken care of everything. Waiting in my room was a welcome package with a custom Cosmo T-shirt, a sweater, jeans, and other items. I had already received cologne, toiletries, and a letter in the mail back home, but seeing more of it waiting in New York made the whole thing feel even more ridiculous.

For a twenty-two-year-old martial arts instructor from Alaska, it was surreal.

That night I went exploring. I walked through Times Square, took in the lights and crowds, and eventually stopped by a nightclub called the China Club. Like the club in Los Angeles, I did not stay long.

I had a big day coming.

The next morning started early.
Really early.

Around five in the morning we were told to put on our Cosmopolitan shirts. Each shirt had our state printed on the back.

Mine said:

ALASKA

Then we started walking toward Rockefeller Plaza.

This was the Today Show.

The same show millions of people watched every morning.

And somehow I was there because of Cosmopolitan.

The kid who got bullied.
The kid from Alaska.

The guy running dojos and DJing clubs.

Now standing in New York City before sunrise wearing a Cosmo shirt.
The whole thing still did not feel real.

Before the show started they handed us musical instruments.
Not to play.

To carry out to the band.

The band that morning was the Goo Goo Dolls.
Again…

Completely ridiculous.

Then another crew showed up.

VH1.
They started interviewing all the bachelors one at a time asking everyone the same question:

"What is your favorite contemporary song?"

Most of the answers were safe.
Polished.
Normal.

Then they got to me.

Being a DJ, I just said what popped into my head.

"The Thong Song."

The whole group exploded.

"Oh yeah!"

The host stopped.

"really?"

I nodded.

Somewhere out there that clip probably still exists.

I have never found it.
But I know it happened.

After The Today Show, they took us to FAO Schwarz.
For people that never experienced it back then, it was not just a toy store.
It was the toy store.

The place was massive.

One of the other bachelors was a boxer, so naturally we ended up putting on oversized boxing gloves and messing around.
Then somebody handed me a pair of shoes.

They had wheels in them.
I had never seen anything like them before.
Heelys.

I rolled around a little while cameras filmed.

Someone asked me what I thought.

I answered honestly.

"These kind of suck. I can feel the wheel pushing into my foot."
Someone quickly reminded me I was on camera.

So I stopped.

Turned.

Gave two thumbs up like Tony the Tiger.

"They're great."

The funny thing is I had no idea those shoes would eventually become huge.

At the time, they were just strange shoes with wheels.

And somehow this was still my life now.

New York. Cosmopolitan. Television crews. Toy stores.

And me rolling around Manhattan in Heelys pretending they were the greatest invention ever made.

After FAO Schwarz they took us to Planet Hollywood.

At some point we ended up sitting down eating ice cream.

Cosmopolitan was having us spoon feed ladies ice cream while cameras were around.

I remember sitting there thinking:

What is happening right now?

A few months earlier I was running dojos in Alaska.

Teaching classes.

DJing.

Driving back and forth between Soldotna and Nikiski.

Now I was sitting in Planet Hollywood in New York while Cosmopolitan staff fed me ice cream for magazine coverage.

The whole thing was absurd.

And I loved every minute of it.

The strange thing looking back now is none of it felt like ego.

It felt like curiosity.

Like life had suddenly opened a door and I was just walking through it seeing what was on the other side.

The kid who got bullied.

The guy who almost got buried by avalanches.

The martial arts instructor trying to build dojos in Alaska.

Now sitting in New York because somehow his story had become interesting enough for Cosmopolitan.

Life was getting strange.

In the best possible way.

And it still was not over.

Later that day we were told to head up to the rooftop pool at the hotel. Someone mentioned Victoria's Secret models were coming.

Okay… cool.

We get up there and something immediately feels off. A few minutes later, seven guys walked out wearing matching bikini-style swim outfits. A couple of the bachelors looked uncomfortable. Honestly, I thought it was a little strange too.

So naturally… I came up with a plan.

I leaned over to a couple of the bigger guys and whispered:

"Let's break this party up. I'm going to pretend we're arguing. Throw me in the pool."

The acting started.

Voices got louder.

Next thing I knew, they launched me straight into the water.

As I climbed out, soaked, I looked around and joked:

"Why do you guys always pick on the smallest guy?"

Everybody started laughing.

Then a cameraman walked over.

"That was great," he said. "What's your name?"

I looked at him.

"Who are you?"

"Entertainment Tonight."

Then he smiled.

"You're going to be on TV."

At that point my life had already become ridiculous.

I had gone from dojo owner… to radio DJ… to club DJ… to Cosmopolitan bachelor… and now somehow I was getting tossed into a rooftop pool while Entertainment Tonight filmed it.

Normal had officially left the building.

After the pool, I changed into the gray sweater you see in the photos. Then we were loaded up and taken to the TCL Chinese Theatre for a movie premiere.

The movie was Boys and Girls - Sex Changes Everything

I remember sitting there realizing the people around me weren't just actors on a screen anymore. Behind me were people like Freddie Prinze Jr., Sarah Michelle Gellar, Jason Biggs, and Claire Forlani. A martial arts instructor from Alaska somehow ended up sitting in the middle of Hollywood watching a premiere with celebrities all around him.

Afterward we went to Bowlmor Lanes.

This place was hidden on the third floor of a random building and from the outside you never would have guessed what was inside. The Victoria's Secret models were there. Eventually Freddie Prinze Jr. showed up too.

But the thing that stuck with me most wasn't the celebrities.

It was the paparazzi.

Everywhere he went, cameras followed.

He couldn't bowl.

Couldn't move.

Couldn't just exist.
Flash.
Flash.
Flash.

And for the first time I remember thinking:

That looks exhausting.

People chase fame their whole lives, but standing there watching it up close changed something for me.

I realized fame might give you visibility…
…but it can also take your freedom.

The next day I decided to try something completely random.
I went to a casting office.

At that point, my life already felt surreal anyway, so why not? Martial arts instructor. Dojo owner. DJ. Cosmopolitan bachelor.

The guy behind the desk looked like he had stepped out of an old gangster movie. Feet up. Cigar. Completely relaxed.

He looked at me and said:

"You're good kid. Reeaall gooood."

Then he asked:
"How much time you got?"

"I leave tomorrow," I told him.

He shook his head.

"If you had one more day, I could get you into a Christmas movie. I owe a friend a favor."

So that seemed like the end of it.

Except life wasn't done.

The next morning my flight was delayed.

Fog.

An entire extra day.

I immediately called him.

And he kept his word.

I ended up on the set of *Never Again*, starring Jeffrey Tambor and Jill Clayburgh. You can see me for maybe a two seconds holding a fake drink.

That was it.
No huge role.
No Hollywood breakthrough.

Just another impossible little detour in a life that already felt like it was refusing to stay inside one lane.

That whole New York and California stretch almost feels unreal.

Cosmopolitan.

Today Show.
Entertainment Tonight.

Movie premieres.

Planet Hollywood.

Hollywood Hills.

Now a movie set.

All while I still had two dojos waiting for me back in Alaska.

New York felt like a preview of a world I didn't know existed.

A martial arts instructor from Alaska somehow ended up on television, walking through Times Square, attending movie premieres, standing on sets, and meeting people whose lives felt completely different from mine.

At twenty-two, life felt wide open.

The dojos were staballized.
The future looked massive.

Everything seemed possible.

What I didn't realize was that while my world was expanding personally, the economic reality back home was already beginning to shift.
I just couldn't see it yet.

The Numbers Start Changing

At first, the changes were subtle.

That's how economic shifts usually happen. Not all at once. Not with some dramatic announcement where everybody suddenly panics overnight. It starts quietly. A student drops. Then another. A parent says they need to "pause for a little while." Someone else says work had slowed down.

Another family quietly disappears without explanation.
Soldotna and the surrounding areas depended heavily on a few industries: fishing, tourism, and oil. Around that time all three seemed to run into problems at nearly the same time. Fishing slowed. Tourism softened. Oil restructuring and uncertainty started affecting families. People lost jobs.

Money became uncertain.

I wasn't looking at statistics. I was watching it happen student by student. Enrollment by enrollment. Conversation by conversation. When families become uncertain financially, martial arts becomes a luxury expense, and luxuries are usually among the first things to go.

The timing made everything harder because while the economy was tightening, my vision was still expanding. The schools had stabilized. Momentum still existed. I was still thinking forward. But the environment around me had already started moving in another direction.

The Nikiski location had originally been an unbelievable deal. Around sixteen hundred square feet for roughly two hundred dollars a month.

At the time it felt like I had found hidden treasure. Enough room to grow. Enough room to dream. Enough room to build something bigger.

Then everything changed.

About a year later, the lease situation shifted. Then the deal that had made Nikishki possible disappeared.

Overnight the numbers no longer worked.

The room was still the same
The students were stilll there

But the foundation underneath it had changed.

I moved into another space. This one was around two thousand square feet with two giant twenty-five-foot bay doors. At first it still felt like momentum. Another move. Another rebuild. Another push forward. That had already become my pattern in life.

Adjust. Adapt. Keep moving.

But this time the math started changing.

Expenses climbed. Student retention became harder. The local economy kept tightening. I was still teaching. Still pushing. Still trying to outwork the problem.

But eventually there comes a point where effort alone cannot overpower reality.

I started seeing the writing on the wall months before everything finally ended. That's one of the hardest parts about entrepreneurship. You often know the storm is coming before everyone else does. You see the trend lines. The missing students. The quieter phones. The bills stacking differently.

And you keep hoping you can reverse it before the wave fully hits.

Failure doesn't happen all at once.
At least not real failure.
Real failure arrives slowly first. Quietly. A feeling in your stomach. Tension. Anxiety building low while your brain keeps trying to convince itself things will somehow turn around. Then disbelief starts. Then shock. Then eventually something worse:

Acceptance.

By late August of 2000, I knew the fight was over.

I had tried everything I knew how to do. Expanded locations. Added programs. Taught more classes. Worked harder. Adjusted constantly. But the numbers kept moving the wrong direction.
And numbers don't care how passionate you are.
The hardest part wasn't the physical work. It was emotional. Because I wasn't just losing a business. I felt like I was losing myself.I had built those schools from almost nothing. A $1,500 signature loan. A bouncing aerobics floor. Long drives. Risk. Faith. Work. And for a while it worked.

That's what made the collapse hurt so much.

If it had failed immediately, maybe it would have been easier to accept. But I had already tasted success. Already expanded. Already experienced momentum. I knew what the dream looked like when it was alive.

That's what made watching it die so painful.

There was no dramatic ending either. No speech. No final class. I quietly put up CLOSED signs.

That was it.

What else was there to say?

People see instructors teaching classes and think passion alone keeps places alive.

It doesn't.

Rent matters.
Economics matter.
Timing matters.

And sometimes forces bigger than you all move at once.

Fishing slowed.
Tourism slowed.
Oil restructuring affected families.

Students disappeared for reasons completely outside my control.

At first I blamed myself for everything.

Honestly…

Part of me still does.

Whatever It Takes

When the dojos closed, life didn't stop long enough for me to process any of it.

That's the strange thing about failure. People imagine dramatic movie scenes where someone sits alone thinking deeply about life while sad music plays in the background.

Real failure feels different.

Bills still exist.
You still need food.
You still need a plan.

So after the shock, anxiety, and disbelief settled enough for me to think straight, survival mode took over.

I started selling Kirby vacuum cleaners.

The transition almost feels absurd. One minute I'm running martial arts schools, teaching classes, DJing clubs, and trying to build something in Alaska.

The next minute I'm knocking on doors selling vacuum cleaners.

But at that point in my life, pride didn't matter anymore.
Survival did.

And honestly, the job taught me a lot.

Selling Kirby vacuums wasn't easy either. You had to communicate quickly. Read people quickly. Handle rejection constantly. Stay mentally sharp while doors closed in your face over and over again.

Most people couldn't handle it very long.

I actually became pretty decent at it.

Not only did I sell, I ended up recruiting three other people into the company who collectively sold around ten Kirbys themselves.

Even in a completely different environment, I still found myself building.
Teaching.
Motivating.

That instinct never really left me.

Then came one of the strangest full-circle moments of my life.

The company offered a prize for anyone that sells 10 Kirbys overall.

I could either take:
$1,500 cash

or

a Kirby vacuum.

And somehow the number hit me immediately.
$1,500.

The exact same amount as the signature loan that launched my first dojo.
Same number.

Different life.

Different chapter.

Most people probably would have taken the cash.

I took the Kirby.

I knew one day I would teach again and I could use to clean my dojos in the future.

At the time, maybe part of me still believed in building instead of just surviving.

Or maybe life just has a strange sense of humor sometimes.

Either way, that moment stuck with me because it felt symbolic.

Like life quietly reminding me:

You're not finished rebuilding yet.

Top Gun Dreams

Like a lot of kids growing up in the eighties and nineties, I had dreams too. Top Gun was everywhere.

Jets. Speed. Pilots. The music. The confidence. It made flying feel larger than life. For a while I thought maybe that would be me one day. Maybe I would fly. Maybe I would do something connected to aviation. I didn't know what yet. I just knew it pulled at something inside me.

At the same time, karate was already pulling just as hard.

I was teaching. Building. Chasing goals. Running schools. Trying to create something of my own before I was old enough to realize how difficult that actually was. Martial arts had already become part of my identity, even if I didn't fully understand where it was taking me yet.

Life was moving fast.
The dojos had stabilized.
The future looked massive.
Everything still felt possible.

It is strange how life leaves clues long before you understand what they mean. At the time, I thought the aviation dream might have passed. I thought maybe that path had gone somewhere else.

I was wrong.

I still ended up around aircraft.

Just not the ones I imagined.

And when the time came to choose, I could have picked almost anything.

I chose Blackhawks.

Joining the Army was not some random decision.
It was another path forward.
Another challenge.
Another way to grow.
And, I was curious where it would lead.

The military offered structure, opportunity, training, travel, and purpose. You could learn skills, build a future, and become part of something bigger than yourself. Standing there looking at possibilities, the list seemed endless.

I could have chosen almost anything.

There were paths into intelligence.
Technical fields.
Other aviation roles.

Plenty of options that probably looked better on paper.

But one thing kept pulling at me.

Blackhawks.

Maybe it was the aircraft, the mission or maybe it was the kid who still remembered Top Gun and never completely let go of the idea of aviation.

Whatever it was, that was the one.

Blackhawks.

That became the target.

At the time, I had no idea how much that decision would matter to me later and those wings would end up meaning far more than the training itself.

Because eventually they would leave my uniform.

And end up somewhere else.

The recruiter laid everything out.

Opportunities.
Training.
Careers.
Different paths.

The Army could take you almost anywhere if you were willing to do the work.

Standing there, I remember thinking about the possibilities. There were practical choices. Safe choices. Paths that probably made more sense.

I ignored them.
I wanted aviation.
I wanted Blackhawks.

That was it.

No debate.
No backup plan.

Just Blackhawks.

The strange thing is aviation had already crossed my path years earlier. Back in high school I had actually taken aviation maintenance classes. Yes, my school offered it.

At the time it just felt interesting. Another thing to learn. Another skill.

I never thought much about it afterward.

Looking back now, it feels like one of those little breadcrumbs life leaves behind long before you understand where they lead.

First Top Gun.
Then aviation maintenance.
Now Blackhawks.
The paperwork moved forward.
The commitment became real.

And somewhere in the middle of all that excitement, I still didn't understand what I was really signing up for.

I thought I was joining the Army.

What I was actually joining was transformation.

But first, they had to be earned.

Basic at Fort Benning

Enlisted into the Army in December of 2000 and was off to Basic Training at Fort Benning, Georgia in January of 2001.

Home of the Infantry. Welcome to Camp Hell.

This place was no joke and I'm sure it was lighter on recruits by the time people read this, but not by much. These days soldiers get their cell phones on Sundays.

Wait… what?

Yes, you heard that right.

Times have changed.

But this timeline would become epic in the way it all unfolded.

Here I was:

Martial artist. Former dojo owner. Cosmopolitan bachelor somehow down on his luck. Vacuum cleaner salesman trying to make a calculated move with my life.

My favorite movies growing up were The Karate Kid and Top Gun. One was about discipline. The other was about flight. Looking back now, I guess I never really escaped either dream.

I did not have the math scores or the uncorrected eyesight to fly jets the way I originally imagined, but by the time I sat down at the recruiter's office, I already knew what I wanted.

Life is what you make it.

I told them I wanted helicopters.

Blackhawks.
If I had to learn how to fix them first and work my way into aviation later, then so be it.

I had started over once already.
Here we go again.

Now it was time to build myself.

The bus ride in felt different.

Not exciting.
Quiet.

The kind of quiet where everyone is thinking but nobody is talking.

Outside the windows Georgia rolled by.
Inside, everybody was carrying some version of their old life with them for the last few minutes they still had it.

That ride was the last moment between two lives.

Because once those doors opened, civilian life started disappearing fast.

I remember stepping off the bus and taking it all in.

Fort Benning.
Home of the Infantry.
Camp Hell.
The name fit.

This place was built to break routines and rebuild people.

And it started immediately.

The Army did not care that I had owned dojos.

It did not care that I taught martial arts.

It definitely did not care that I had somehow ended up in Cosmopolitan.

Everyone started at the same place.
Haircuts. Paperwork. Shots.

Waiting.

More waiting.

Civilian life was getting peeled away one layer at a time.

And maybe, that was the point.

A few months earlier I had been walking through New York wondering what came next.

Now, I was standing at Fort Benning holding everything I still was while the Army quietly started taking it apart.

The first few hours blurred together. Move here. Stand there. Wait. Move again. It felt strange how quickly time changed because minutes felt long while entire hours disappeared.

Little by little the outside world started getting farther away. Family. Friends. Normal life. Civilian Corey. That version of me was still there, but Fort Benning had already started introducing me to someone else.

The barracks finally came into view. This was no longer a recruiter's office, a movie scene, or imagination. This was where we would sleep, wake up, train, fail, adapt, and become whatever the Army intended us to become. Camp Hell had an address now.

And somehow that made it more real.

The first night felt strange.

You were surrounded by people, yet somehow everything still felt quiet in your own head. The noise of the day was over, but now your mind had time to catch up to where you were.

Fort Benning.
Georgia.

Thousands of miles from Alaska.

Somewhere between the waiting, the movement, and the chaos, it finally hit me.

The kid who got pushed around in school. The kid who kept rebuilding himself. The kid from Alaska who once wondered what his future would be had made it all the way here.

And now the real work was about to begin.

Sometimes rebuilding your life starts with competely surrendering the identity you thought you were suppose to have.

Camp Hell

The barracks finally came into view.

This was no longer a recruiter's office, a movie scene, or imagination. This was where we would sleep, wake up, train, fail, adapt, and become whatever the Army intended us to become.

Camp Hell had an address now.

And somehow that made it more real.
The barracks were exactly what they needed to be. Rows of bunks. Gear. Soldiers trying to figure out where they belonged and what came next. Everyone was new, and everyone was pretending they understood what was happening.

Most of us didn't.

This was Reception Battalion, or week zero. It didn't officially count as Basic Training yet, but it counted to me. This was where civilian life started getting peeled away before the real storm arrived.

Like I said before, bring cologne? Good luck. Gone.

Bring a lock with a key? Bad idea. They take the key at the beginning of Basic and you don't get it back until the end.

Bring a disposable camera? Put it at the top of your duffle bag and thank me later.

We were assigned bunks and battle buddies. Mine was seventeen years old, so I claimed the bottom bunk immediately. He didn't seem too bothered by it, and honestly, I wasn't asking.

As I laid my head down, I noticed something valuable someone had left behind.

Staring straight ahead. I saw it.
A digital alarm clock.

I grabbed that thing instantly.

In Basic Training, small advantages matter.
That alarm clock became one of mine.

My bunk was the fourth one on the right when you walked in. Two rows. Bathrooms near the stairs. Drill sergeants on the other side. The room itself was probably forty by sixty feet, but somehow it felt much smaller once everyone and everything was packed inside.

Then the drill sergeants came in.

That is when the room changed.

The first drill sergeant came in and had everyone at attention almost instantly. He was hispanic and seemed nice.

We knew what we were there for, and everyone took it seriously. The room got quiet fast.

He spoke for maybe five or ten minutes.

Then another drill sergeant came in.

Then, the Black drill sergeant showed up. His tone felt lighter at first. Different.

Then the final drill sergeant arrived.

Short. White. Stocky. Braces. Almost crazy energy.

He felt like the leader of the cycle.

Looking back now, it is funny how quickly people start studying personalities when pressure enters the room.

Who is strict? Who jokes? Who do you avoid? Who notices everything?

You start learning fast because the environment demands it.

And whether we realized it yet or not…

Camp Hell had officially started interviewing us.

Hand to Hand Combat

Around the fifth week is when we started hand-to-hand combat training. This was also probably when peak testosterone was kicking in and everyone thought they were a badass.

One night we were marched out to a field while it was still dark. It was near mid-March and we watched the drill sergeant demonstrate ground fighting, jiu-jitsu, and grappling.
I was taking all of it in.

Memorizing methods and techniques to possibly use later on down the road.

The next morning after a workout and breakfast, we were out in the grass practicing reversals.

One guy mounts another. You hook their leg and reverse positions.

Simple.

The sun was nearing high noon without a cloud in the sky.

Deep blue backdrop.

I did the reversal once and it was easy.
Then, my partner reversed me.
Now I'm staring directly into the sun. Again

The next time I closed my eyes while doing the reversal.

A drill sergeant saw it instantly.

"Are you sleeping, Private Green?"

"No drill sergeant."

"It looked like you were sleeping."

A few moments later I was back on bottom with my partner when the drill sergeant said:

"Let's see if you know what you're doing."

He pulled the other soldier off of me, loosely slinging him and then mounted me himself.

"Let's see what you got."

I reversed him.

His eyes got REAL BIG.

"GET OFF ME, BOY!"

I got off him immediately.

As he stood up and started walking away, my hispanic drill sergeant said something I wasn't expecting.

"Oh, that's Private Green. He knows Ka-Ra-Te."

Great, I thought.

My battle buddy let me down.

On day one the drill sergeants told everyone to tell their battle buddy all about themselves.

Well…

They just got the intel they needed.

The head hand to hand combat drill sergeant who had mounted me stopped and looked back.

"Is that true, Private Green?"

"Nooo drillll serge-ant."

Then the Hispanic drill sergeant jumped in.
"No drill sergeant, that's private Green. He's a black belt. He knows Ka-Ra-Te."

"Is that true, Private Green?"

"Nooo drillll serge-ant."

Most of the time it's just safer to say no.

The drill sergeant took a few more steps, stopped, looked back over his left shoulder and said:

"Hey Green… wanna play?"

I replied instantly.

"Bring it on, drill sergeant."

Now I know most people would never say something like that. How? I've been asking for 25 years when I share this story.

The truth is, I wasn't trying to be disrespectful.

I just wasn't scared.

Without wasting a second he turned around, grabbed the guy who had been on top of me by the belt loops and the back of his shirt and literally tossed him aside.

I can still see his arms and legs flailing against that deep blue sky.

Then the drill sergeant mounted me differently than the night before.

He pinned my hands above my head.

Perfect. I love this move. I remember teaching it to high school girls back at the high school's on the Kenai Peninsula. It was one of my signature favorite moves of all time.

I tucked in my left knee to brace him and stretched out my right leg.

He looked me dead in the eyes.

I looked right back at him.

"Are you ready, Private Green?"

Grinning I said,

"Are you ready, drill sergeant?"

You elevate both wrists 1/16", sweep the arms down in a downward snow-angel motion.

My right leg drove forward with everything I had, straight into his behind.

Launch sequence. INITIATED.

Usually people land on top of you. So you bring your hands back in to your guard.

But this time, I made him fly.

To this day, it is still the best launch I have ever made on anyone.

While he was still descending,

I jumped on top of him like a cat.

Top mount. I go for an top mount arm bar because you cannot hit the drill sergeants. Or you are not suppose to.

So I go for the armbar. He Escapes.

He goes for an armbar. I Escape.

Back and forth.

I accidentally landed a punch.

I did the Jazz hands apology.

He never gained control.

He then says to me, "Stop, stop! Do you see how out of shape this private is?

This is the talking trash about conditioning while buying time.
I stay mounted. Yes, he is still under me.

The head hand-to-hand combat drill sergeant slowly starts putting his left hand on my shirt to get a grip.

I recognized this move instantly.
It was from the night before.

I grabbed him by his right shoulder and his left hand.

Then,I went to the right and put my legs around his neck.

I had his arm trapped between my legs and elevated my hips towards the sky.

He managed to escape and he swings his legs around to my neck.

Then I see.
and think to myself...
I have an issue.

I stand up and start twisting his feet off of my neck.

Suddenly.

The other drill sergeants step in and pull us apart.

Done.

Later another soldier would actually choke out a drill sergeant with his own shirt.

I remember thinking,
"Shoot, I didn't know that was allowed or I would have done that too."

Once we are dismissed from formation, this one guy was so estatic about what he just witnessed that he totally wanted a piece of the action. And, as they say, Honestly, I wasn't interested. At all. I was done. Or at least I thought I was.

In my mind, I was just trying to process what just happened. I just dominated the head to hand combat drill sergeant and I didn't start it but I darn sure did finish it.

I stood up to a man I never in my wildest dreams thought would have ever would be part of my timelline.

This reminds me of my father. He was a man that wanted his own sons to stand up to him when they turned 18 to prove that they were a man.

I think all of that emotion, stress, success, loss, frustration, glory, building and rebuilding of myself is exactly what I needed to be resilent in the future because the future was not the path I could have ever predicted.

I hear him. He won't stop. I try to ignore him

"Hey, You wanna wrasle?"

"No, I'm good."

"No, You wanna wrasle when we get back to the barracks?"

"Does it look like I want to wrasle when we get back to the barracks?
I just fought the head hand to hand combat drill sergeant.
No, I do not Want To Wrestle."

"Oh Come On! It will be fun!"

"No"

We are still walking to the barracks when this all transpires.

Then, he asks again. I give him my same response. No.

We are at the base of the steps now. We have 3 flights of stairs to go.

He asks.

"No!"

"Please!"

We are at the top of the stairs and if you have been keeping count like I have, that is 5 times. I was counting then too.

Would you believe that this man asked again for a 6th time. I gave him my same response but this time in my mind I thought about it. I said to myself, if he asks a 7th time, I will say, "Yes."

Guess what?

He did.

I said, "Hey just give me a minute okay?"

He said, "okay."

He seemed a little pumped up.

And...

I was about to deflate his ego.

The Army Wrestler

When I walked out into the middle of the barracks, everyone was already forming a half circle around us waiting to see what would happen.

They wanted to see how I would handle a wrestler.

I noticed immediately that he still had socks on. Big mistake for him.

The floor had just been freshly waxed.

By ME. I took pride in my floor. You could see your face in the reflection.

I took my socks off.

My feet gripped the floor perfectly.

Almost like Spider-Man compared to the slick waxed floor.

I call it Spidey feet.

I still had my BDU pants and shirt on.

I walk out there with 50 men in attendance watching, waiting to see what was about to go down.

I didn't ask for any of this. But I had to show them all that I was no one to be messed with. I just want to help people and not be attacked.

We circled for maybe four seconds in wrestling stances before he shot for my legs.

I sprawled immediately. i pushed my legs back and put my weight on hm.

Alwhile.

My right hand was controlling the back of his neck.
simutaneously I applied my left hand to the upper part of his right arm.

I was controlling him and I have the upper hand.

I closed the distance and wrapped him up with his own momentum with his own arms.

A move I have never done before in my life.

He kept trying to drive forward, but I had complete leverage over him. My spidey feet gave me maximum control over positioning and direction.

Then I started thinking.

Well... I can't hit him.

I can't choke him.
Otherwise I could end up in serious trouble.

So... I improvised.

I looked over and saw all the metal military bed frames lined up neatly along the barracks wall.

I slid him over and pinned his neck between my knee and the vertical support frame of the bed.

The same kind of metal frame every soldier remembers from Basic Training.

I gently placed his neck up against the metal bar.

I put my knee into his neck and starting driving the entire bed with his neck.

The metal scraping sound, you could hear it echo in the barracks room.

The men I am sure they were shocked because they were probably thinking, this wasn't in the training manual or hand to hand combats sessions.

He got furious.

He sounded like Beavis when he got mad, so I released him.

That's when he picked me up and slammed me.

By this point in my life I know some Judo.
So I judo slapped the floor just at the proper moment.

I was laughing. This was actual kinda fun. I felt invincible.

It didn't hurt, but I immediately realized something important.

He wasn't playing anymore.

He was trying to hurt me.

As he laid me on my right side, he was trying to choke me out. That is when I prepared my left hand two finger jugular strike preparation technique. And yes, I prepared to strike his jugular if I absolutely had to.

Before things escalated further, the other soldiers jumped in and pulled us apart.

I stood up immediately and reached my hand out.

"Hey, are you okay man?"

He slapped my hand away. "Get away from me."

I waited maybe thirty seconds and tried again.

"Hey, you okay?"

"Yeah, I'm okay."

Then I said:

"I told you I didn't want to wrestle."

"Yeah," he replied.

"I got it now."

Then the biggest guy in the barracks asked:

"Hey Green, you wanna wrasle?"

I looked at him and asked:

"Can I punch and kick you?"

"No."

"Then we're not wrasling because I know if you get your hands on me, I'm toast."

Obstacle Course

The obstacle courses at Fort Benning reminded me of growing up in Alaska.

The obstacles were a combination of agility, strength, balance, fitness, finesse, and perseverance.

I was pretty quick on the course, just like many of the other soldiers. Sometimes I would catch up to the person ahead of me only to stand there waiting my turn for the next obstacle.

The obstacle that stood out the most was the giant ladder climb.
This wasn't your normal Home Depot ladder.
This thing was built out of stripped tree trunks with two-by-fours nailed across them as steps.

Each rung got farther apart the higher you climbed.

The last rung was a bugger for a five-foot-seven-and-a-half-inch man.

You had to jump.

And you better not miss.

I remember looking down and seeing the foam pad and sawdust below thinking:

Yeah… like that's really going to help.

It reminded me of a cartoon where someone dives into a tiny cup of water.

Once you descended the ladder, you had to transition onto a rope with no harness.

Just a net below to catch the people who didn't have it in them.

Did I make it?

Yep.

One day while training on the obstacle course, I somehow cut my arm without noticing it.

I was only on a second-level obstacle.

Nothing too crazy.

To get down we had to slide down a rope.

Unfortunately, the rope lined up perfectly with the cut on my arm.

That's how the infection started.

That night I felt extremely hot.

By morning I knew I was in trouble.

I had a 104-degree fever.

The drill sergeant wasn't pleased because this was our third of five road marches and I was about to miss three days because I could barely function.

They didn't give me a ride to the hospital.

They made me walk.

I'd guess it was somewhere between a quarter mile and half a mile.

That walk was one of the hardest journeys I had experienced up to that point in my life.

When I finally arrived, they took their time admitting me.

Eventually, I ended up hooked up to IVs and medication for dehydration and the infection.

I remember a nurse coming in with a giant pill.

I told her:

"I can't swallow that."

She replied instantly:

"I didn't ask you to."

By the second day I was already feeling much better.

Technically I still wasn't out of the woods.

A few of us noticed the staff wasn't paying much attention to the soldiers and realized the BX was nearby.

So naturally…

We snuck out.

We removed insignia from our uniforms and went to get supplies that weren't allowed during Basic Training because of their dumb rules.

We made it back without getting caught.

Others heard about our little adventure later and tried doing the same thing.

They got caught.

I know whatever happened afterward wasn't good.

The next day a Royal Air Force officer came in asking for two volunteers.

I already knew never to volunteer for anything in the Army unless you knew exactly what it was.

Two soldiers asked:

"What are you going to do?"

The officer replied:

"We're going to put something in your nose and pull it back out."

"Will it hurt?"

"Oh yeah."

A couple hours later they came back holding their noses in pain and immediately regretting their decision.

Eventually I returned to my unit.

The guys missed me.

As I returned to the barracks, the guys had a different perspective of me now and wasn't of weakness.

It was of respect and strength.

They looked at me probably as an Alpha but I was just trying to get through Basic like everyone else.

I just kept being tested.

The question was raised about me missing a road march and I told them, "Doctors orders."

I didn't owe anyone, anything.

They knew that.

The respect grew and the tensions eased from that point until we learned that we would have the opportunity to hit each other with gigantic Q-Tips.

Another day we all knew was coming.
Nobody talked about it much.

We had other things on our minds.

Lightning Rod

The first thing we had to do after marching several miles into the training area was dig foxholes with our terrible Army-issued shovels.

My battle buddy wanted to sleep.

The foxhole wasn't going to dig itself.

No matter what I said, I couldn't motivate him to help.

So I dug the entire thing myself.

About four feet deep and wide enough for two people to fit comfortably.

Was I exhausted?

Absolutely.

Then, we had to pitch the tent and dig trenches around it to redirect rainwater if a storm came.

Not a cloud in the sky at the time, but they warned us it would "bahoove" us to dig trenches anyway.

Almost nobody did it.

I did.

Even exhausted, I kept pushing.

After everything was set up, we were told to grab our rifles.

Whenever the rifles came out, something was about to happen.

As night arrived, so did a nasty storm.

Lightning.

Thunder.

The whole show.

This was around April of 2001.

The drill sergeants already knew the weather was going to be bad all night and into the next day.

They assembled us in formation.

"Alright everyone," the drill sergeant yelled. "Put your rifle in your right hand. Put your left hand on the person next to you in formation. Now lift your rifle into the air."

We followed instructions.

"Congratulations," he shouted!
"You are now one giant mother****ing lightning rod."

We all looked around wondering what in the world we had gotten ourselves into.

After what felt like forever he finally ordered:
"Order arms!"

Then we were told to get back to our tents, pack our gear, and prepare to load up into the deuce-and-a-halfs back to the barracks.

As I entered my tent, I could hear soldiers complaining their stuff was soaked.

Meanwhile my trench system had worked.

I changed into warm clothes inside the tent while listening to the rain hammer everything outside.

Once I stepped back out into the storm, the water didn't even feel cold anymore.

I climbed into the diesel-smelling deuce-and-a-half smiling the whole ride back.

Pugil Sticks

Pugil sticks were basically the Army's version of giant Q-tips designed for soldiers to beat the crap out of each other with.

By this point in Basic Training, everyone had developed reputations. The guy whose bunk was immediately next to mine had become known as the king of shining boots. He took enormous pride in them, and the drill sergeants noticed too.

His boots were so polished you could practically use them as mirrors.

One day the drill sergeants made him wear those perfectly polished boots straight through the mud.

You could see the heartbreak all over his face afterward.

He immediately went to work cleaning and restoring them again.

At first we didn't really get along that well, but when it came time for pugil sticks, we chose each other.

We both fought hard.

Blocking.

Swinging.

Landing shots at nearly the exact same time.

Neither one of us backed down.

The only thing that stopped us was the bell ending the match.
It was ruled a draw.

After that, we respected each other and became respected and good friends for the rest of Basic Training.

Drill Sergeant Morgan

One of the craziest drill sergeant moments happened around two in the morning.

The same crazy white drill sergeant Drill Sergeant Morgan from Fort Benning January 2001, decided to pull a prank on the soldiers.

He was wearing his BDU uniform and Kevlar helmet, but hanging down from the sides were chains that looked almost like braids.

The lights were completely off and everyone was asleep.

I've always been a pretty light sleeper thankfully, because what happened next, was something I'll never forget.

As I laid there pretending to sleep, I heard the chains gently clinking while the drill sergeant moved through the barracks with another person carrying a flashlight.

I noticed immediately the orange stopper on the rifle and knew it wasn't loaded.

The drill sergeant was walking around poking random soldiers just to see how they would react.

Not everybody.

Just certain soldiers he selected.

I already knew he was coming for me.
I later realized I was probably his fifth pick that night.
I heard him whisper quietly before he reached my bunk.

"Green..."

He came to the right side of my bed.

I was ready.

The moment he poked my right rib cage with the rifle, I reacted instantly.

In karate, we have a movement called kakete, or grabbing hands.

I hooked the end of the rifle and yanked hard while rolling left out of bed acting like some kind of grizzly bear waking up angry from hibernation.
Heavy breathing.
Aggressive movement.

Then I calmly stopped.

"Oh… it's just you, drill sergeant."

Then I climbed right back into bed and went to sleep.

He left after my encounter.

I guess he got a little more than he bargained for.

Pizza Party

The pizza party at the Home of the Infantry was almost unheard of.

Cell phones barely existed yet and life in Basic Training was repetitive, structured, and honestly boring at times.

So when they asked who wanted to be in charge of waxing the floors, I immediately volunteered.

Not because I loved cleaning floors.
Because I knew it wouldn't be boring.

I had never operated one of those old-school waxing machines before and figured it would at least give me something interesting to learn.

Every chance I got when nothing else was happening, I worked on those floors.

Somehow I knew the irony would eventually show itself.
A karate guy obsessively waxing floors.

Sure enough, one day they announced there was going to be a competition.

Whichever platoon had the shiniest floor would win a pizza party.

At Fort Benning.
At the Home of the Infantry.
Pizza and Coke.

No joke.

I took enormous pride in that floor. I worked on it since day one. Every Sunday building up that floor.

You could literally see your reflection in it just like my neighbor's boots.

The night they announced the winners, we won.

That pizza party changed how people looked at me.

For a brief moment, I was redeemed and respected on another level.

Not because I could fight.

Because I cared enough to outwork everyone at something small.

Soldier Of The Month

Shortly after the pizza party, another opportunity appeared.

Soldier of the Month.

The platoon leader Paden, another soldier, and myself found ourselves sitting together trying to understand exactly what Soldier of the Month even involved.

Back in high school I had been Cadet of the Year in JROTC three consecutive years and placed second out of more than a thousand cadets twice. I still have the certificates framed. One says Corey Hill. The other says Corey Bishop.

Long story.

When the drill sergeant entered the room, the atmosphere changed instantly.

He had me stand up.

Then he just started yelling directly in my face. Spit flying everywhere.

I kept subtly moving my head trying not to get spit directly into my eyes and mouth.

That tiny movement was enough.

"Nope Green. You're out. "That was it. No second chance.

Just like that, Soldier of the Month, disappeared.

At least for now.

The strange thing about the Army is that opportunities have a way of coming back around.

Sometimes when you least expect them.
And sometimes after you have already accepted they are gone.

The last day of graduation finally arrived.

I remember marching with my platoon and genuinely enjoying the moment.
We had made it.

At least most of us. Not everyone who starts Fort Benning finishes with all fifty-two.

We did.

Mostly.

The strange part was watching the drill sergeants.

Some of them could barely look me in the eyes while saying goodbye.
Then my Hispanic drill sergeant, the same one who got me exposed during hand-to-hand combat by telling everyone I was a black belt, looked away to his right with tears in his eyes and quietly said:

"Get out of here, Green."

That moment stayed with me.
Because somewhere along the way we had stopped being recruits.
We had become soldiers.

After graduation my parents took me out to eat.
Then they told me three things.
First: My dad was officially disabled.
Second: My mom was officially disabled too.
Third: One of my highest-ranking students from Alaska had died. Darby Rouswell. It was an accidental self terminate.

He had suffered from hiccups for weeks and became desperate trying to make them stop. He used a plastic bag and accidentally suffocated himself.
I didn't really have time to process any of it. AIT was waiting.

Part one of my Army journey was over.
Part two was about to begin.

Orders to Fort Eustis,

AIT training waited at Fort, Eustis, Virginia.

Black Hawk helicopter Repair school

UH-60

Basic Training was over.

Fort Benning had stripped everybody down to the basics. Sweat. Dirt.

Push-ups. Sand. Mud. Repetition. Somewhere in the middle of all that, fifty-two strangers had become a platoon.

Then just like that… it was over.

Orders came down.

Fort Eustis, Virginia.
Blackhawk Helicopter Repair School.

The next phase.

My parents drove me there.

I remember the ride feeling strangely quiet. Not awkward quiet. Heavy quiet.

Basic had changed me.

I wasn't the same person who got on that bus headed to Fort Benning months earlier. The dojo owner version of me felt farther away now. The guy selling Kirby vacuums felt farther away too.

Now I was a soldier headed toward helicopters.
The ride felt long, but underneath everything else there was excitement. Because this was childhood dream territory now.

Top Gun dreams had turned into rotor blades.

I wasn't flying yet.

But I was getting closer.

And somewhere in those hours between Fort Benning and Fort Eustis, another identity shift happened without me realizing it.

I stopped thinking about what I had lost in Alaska.

And started thinking about what I was building next.

When Fort Eustis finally came into view, the atmosphere felt completely different.

Fort Benning was pressure.

Fort Eustis felt possibility.

Blackhawks were waiting.

And I was ready to meet them.

Blackhawk School

I arrived at Fort Eustis one day early instead of taking the extra free day they offered before reporting. At that point,I figured I might as well just get started.

Only four of us from Basic Training had become UH-60 Blackhawk helicopter mechanics:
Powell, Paden, Singleton, and me.
Powell was the biggest physically. Singleton and Paden were taller than me, but I was compact, athletic, and carried years of martial arts training into everything I did.

The moment I stepped into the barracks at Fort Eustis, I knew life had shifted again. Fort Benning was the House of Pain. Fort Eustis felt easy.

There were many more washers and dryers, people were more relaxed, and the chow hall was fully stocked. That alone made me happy.

Fort Benning felt like survival. This felt like progression.

Then came the helicopters.

Seeing the aircraft for the first time felt strangely familar.

Back in high school, I had taken aviation maintainence classes.
At the time, it seemed interesting.

Standing there now, looking at helicopters for real, it felt less random.

But...

Not the flying yet. First came the learning. the tools, systems, procedures, and responsibility and maybe we will have a chance to fly. Nothing was guaranteed. You had to earn your wings.

One thing got drilled into us immediately: accountability. If you removed something from the aircraft, you documented it. If you reinstalled it, you documented it again. Everything mattered because mistakes here didn't just cost money. They could cost lives.

Our first major graded task involved removing and reinstalling a helicopter wheel assembly. This was nothing like changing a tire on a car.

Everything had procedures and documentation.

My partner and I split responsibilities. He handled the physical work while I documented every step.

The problem was simple.

I trusted him too much.
I was writing instead of watching.
We ran out of time.

Out of roughly twelve students, only two groups failed. Mine was one of them. The highest score I could now earn on the retest was seventy percent.

Then came the question:

"Do you want another partner or do you want to do it solo?"

Most people probably would have chosen to partner again.

I didn't.

I chose solo.

The instructors made sure I understood the risk. Doing it alone meant I had to perform the work and document every step myself. If I failed again,

I would lose the MOS entirely.

I wasn't letting somebody else derail childhood dream number two.

We started.

I worked.

I finished.

My former partner didn't.

He got reassigned.

I passed.
But the victory felt strange. I had won, yet somehow it still felt like I had lost something. I went back to the barracks feeling conflicted.
Their perception of me shifted again.

I knew I would eventually have to prove myself all over again.

That opportunity came sooner than expected.

One evening after a long day at the hangar, I was starving. Breakfast had been light and lunch hadn't done much. By dinner I felt like I hadn't eaten all day.

At AIT, anyone who had been there longer than you, even by a week, was considered senior. That mattered to some people.

We lined up outside the chow hall by squad positions. I took first position in second squad instead of first squad.

A soldier immediately came over trying to move me.

Not politely.
Not respectfully.

Just authority for the sake of authority.

Words were exchanged and his tone kept escalating. Then he shoved me with both hands directly in the chest.

I redirected him.

Years of martial arts had taught me that when someone pushes, you don't have to stop the force. You only have to know how to redirect it at the right time.

Simple.

He stumbled sideways.
He came again.

Same result.

Third time.
Same result.

Finally I told him:

"LOOK, I DON'T WANT TO PLAY WITH YOU RIGHT NOW. BESIDES… DRILL SERGEANT IS WATCHING."

That ended it.

At least for the moment.

That night I honestly wondered if I was going to wake up getting hit with soap in a sock or dragged into a fight.

Instead, I woke up and everyone was watching me.

I reached under my pillow.

A used condom.

I lifted it with two fingers and laughed.

"Gross. Is that the best you got?"

Then I walked off.
The soldier never bothered me again.

Around that same time another martial artist and I became friends.

Jose Garcia.

Kung Fu Practitioner

A drill sergeant heard both of us had martial arts backgrounds and gave us four soldiers each to teach for an hour. This was to see who was the better teacher.

Jose taught hand-to-hand combat.

I taught Taikyoku Shodan. A very common kata in karate.

The drill sergeant gave me the win because the kata could be practiced alone.

Jose took it well.
We stayed friends.

That night we sparred in the dark barracks.
We both landed at almost the same time.
Both of us started bleeding.
We looked at each other and agreed:

"Yeah, we should probably stop."

After everything with training, my partner not making it through, and the pressure still waiting back home, I think part of me just wanted a break.

By this point we had earned Gold Status.

Gold Status was awarded for maintaining good standing and performance.

Most soldiers used it to go to Virginia Beach, get drunk, and enjoy a little freedom before coming back to reality.

I had rollerblades and used them all over base because cars and bicycles weren't allowed, but somehow rollerblades were.

Eventually I decided to go too.

I bought Captain Morgan Parrot Bay rum and orange juice, filled my CamelBak with ice and the mixture, and boarded the bus to Virginia Beach. The ride was a few hours long and somewhere along the way I realized I had made a mistake.

By the time the bus arrived, I was already heavily intoxicated.
I stood up and immediately thought:

Uh oh. I am in trouble.

I could barely walk.
I staggered off the bus, wandered around for a while, and eventually got a hotel room.

At some point that night I apparently filled the bathtub with cold water and climbed inside because I later woke up in it completely exhausted.

Lying there, I remember thinking:

Yeah… this isn't my path.

I wasn't an alcoholic.

But I was carrying stress.
Failed businesses. My parents' health.
The uncertainty of life. The pressure of trying to rebuild.
For a brief moment I had drifted toward something that could have become a bad direction.

I decided right there I wasn't going to keep walking that road.

Alcohol wasn't my path.

Training was.
Purpose was.
Mission was.

Gas Chamber

The gas chamber was another unforgettable equalizer.

Going into that chamber was one of the more challenging parts of military training.

The first time through, they had us stand in formation wearing gas masks before eventually ordering us to remove them one by one.

Once your mask came off, you had to state your name, date of birth, and repeat whatever else they wanted while breathing CS gas.

At first the gas hits your eyes and lungs like fire.

Then something strange happens.
Your body almost starts adapting to it.

At least temporarily.
But the absolute worst part wasn't inside the chamber.

It was stepping back outside.

The first breath of fresh air triggered everything.

Mucus and phlegm poured from everyone uncontrollably.
Soldiers bent over with their hands on their knees trying to recover while draining like broken faucets.

Nobody looked tough out there.
Everybody was equal.

The second time through was easier mentally.

Not physically.
Mentally.

Now you knew what was coming.
By this point in AIT, I could feel some of my classmates had me figured wrong.

Then one Friday afternoon the master sergeant gathered everyone together before every jetted off for the golden weekend.

"Alright," the drill sergeant said reluctantly. "Who wants to go to Soldier of the Month board?"

Nobody raised their hand.

I did.

He handed me the study guide.
About four hundred pages.

The board was only a few days away.
Friday. Saturday. Sunday. Monday.
Board on Tuesday.

So I studied.

Every chance I had.

Soldier Of The Month

The study guide was around four hundred pages and I had four days to prepare.

I studied every chance I had. Current events was also part of the test so I had to watch the news and remember any news story that might stick out.

When the board finally happened, I answered each question to the best of my ability. Then came a current event question. It was about a shark attack off the coast of Florida. They asked if I could explain what happened.

"Yes drill sergeant,

An 8 year old boy had his arm severed by the shark. His uncle wrestled the bull shark onto shore. The park ranger shot the shark and the boys arm was pulled out put on ice and the reattached to the kids arm. Drill Sergeant."

I started answering questions and even gave the page numbers where the answers could be found. The drill sergeants laughed quietly and I walked out thinking I had probably blown it.

The next day in the hangar I suddenly heard a drill sergeant yelling:

"WHERE'S PRIVATE GREEN? I NEED TO SPEAK WITH PRIVATE GREEN!"

I walked over.

"Private Green, you won. You are Soldier of the Month. Congratulations!

You now go in front of the brigade. Good luck, son."

The look on my classmates' faces said everything. They had me pegged wrong. There was no reason to say anything. They knew. I knew. And they knew I knew.

The Brigade board came next. I gave it everything I had, but afterward a Master Sergeant pulled me aside and said:

"You had that. You answered more questions correctly than anyone else.

But you didn't say 'drill sergeant' after every response, so they picked another soldier."

Then he looked at me and said:

"I'm putting paperwork in for the 160th if you want it."

The 160th Special Operations Aviation Regiment. Elite level. I answered immediately:

"Yes, master sergeant."

Around the same time the hardship situation with my parents kept getting worse. I went looking for answers and was told to handle it at my duty station. Later I would be told the exact opposite. That contradiction would become one of the most frustrating parts of the entire process.

Celebratory Pizza

After everything that had happened, a celebration felt earned. I had locked in graduation, won Soldier of the Month, and earned respect from people who had underestimated me. I also knew my final PT score wasn't going to change anything at this point, so I relaxed a little.

I ordered pizza. It took almost three hours to arrive on base. I didn't care that I was allergic to milk and cheese. I was celebrating.

The next morning the alarm went off for the final PT test.

I knew immediately I was in trouble.

The pizza had destroyed me.

Push-ups came first.
Normally I could knock out eighty-eight in two minutes
That morning I managed around seventy before my stomach started reminded me of the pizza.
Sit-ups weren't much better and could normally knock out another eighty-eight.

Then came the two-mile run.
Eight laps around the track.

I made it about a mile before I knew things were about to get ugly.

A soldier passed me and smirked.

"Green, you're such a pussy."
Then I threw up.

While running.

I never stopped.
I kept moving and eventually caught him.

Then I passed him.

For the next few laps I stayed ahead.
On the final lap, disaster struck again.

I threw up a second time.
He ran by laughing.

"Like I said, Green, you're such a pussy."

I finished throwing up, dropped the hammer, and sprinted.

I crossed the finish line ahead of him.

Then I looked over and said:

"I threw up twice and still beat you.

Now who's the pussy?"

Fort Campbell

August of 2001 finally arrived. I graduated AIT and received orders to Fort

Campbell, Kentucky.

As Sergeant Barks drove me from the barracks.

I told him that I was Soldier of the Month at Fort Eustis.

He turned and looked at me with his 1980's mustache almost poking me in the face.

"Flight or mechanic?"

"Flight." I answered immediately.

A little while later I walked into my room.

Finally.

Finally, I had a place to call my own.

There wasn't much to it.

Four walls. Brick. White. Cold industrial tile floors with little black streaks running through them. The closet door was broken. No sink. No bathroom. No fridge until I bought one myself.
Just a bed and no roommate, which was unusual and one of the reasons I liked the older barracks so much.

Third floor.

No elevator.

One of the first things I bought that I still use today was a George Foreman grill.

What did I cook?
Steak.
Constantly.

What did I drink?
This was the beginning of my red wine experiences.
Somehow, if you eat steak and sip red wine long enough, the steak starts tasting better and better. At least that's what my brain convinced me of.

The smell started attracting people from all over the top floor.
Neighbors would stop by and offer to buy food.

I never sold any.

Once I got everything organized and settled into a routine, I honestly felt good about the choices I had made up to that point.

For the first time in a long time, life felt stable.

Communication with Alaska was limited.

This was still 2001.

Cell phones weren't what they later became. Pay phones still existed and calling Alaska wasn't cheap.

Every time I talked with my parents though, the situation sounded worse.

From ages eleven through eighteen, I grew up extremely poor.
So poor I never even got a class ring in high school.

That still bothered my mom years later.
I always told her the same thing:
"It's just high school."

I had moved out at nineteen and by twenty-one my parents had moved closer to me.
It made life easier for all of us.

That gave me more time with them after they relocated from Anchorage to Nikiski while I was building the martial arts school in Soldotna.
Then came the phone call after I got settled at Fort Campbell.

My mom explained their living situation was becoming unstable and financially dangerous.

Both of my parents were now officially disabled while I was serving active duty.

Add Alaska winters to that equation and everything felt magnified.

The danger felt real.

Then September 11th happened.

It was one of those calm blue-sky days.

A soldier buddy and I had gone off base while I was still learning my way around Fort Campbell. My car was still in Alaska, so getting around wasn't easy, especially with the helicopter hangars sitting toward the edge of the base.

We were driving around enjoying the day when suddenly the radio interrupted everything:

"This is an emergency news break.
A plane has hit one of the Twin Towers."

My battle buddy and I looked at each other immediately.

"We need to get back to base.

When we returned, security at the gate had completely changed.

Long lines.
ID checks.
Everybody serious.

Tense.

By the time we arrived at the Humvee depot and informally reported in, the second tower had already been hit.

That's when Sergeant Barks looked around and said:

"Ohhh yeah… we're going to war."

At that moment the reality of joining the Army hit me fully.
I realized something else too.

Because of my parents' worsening situation and my pursuit of a hardship discharge, people were eventually going to assume I was trying to get out because of 9/11.

That wasn't true.

My hardship situation had already started before the attacks.

It was real.
It was serious.

It was probably life-saving for my parents.

Some of the people from my unit never came back from deployment.

Others came back different forever.

That thought still sits with me today.

The Spotlight

A few weeks after 9/11, my third oldest brother Derek came to visit me.

Derek is a natural-born carpenter. The last full house he built himself was for country music star, Trace Adkins.

The first thing he wanted to do after arriving wasn't sightseeing.

It was karate.

I was honored.

Here we were in a grassy field next to the old barracks at Fort Campbell, home of the Screaming Eagles.

We were about halfway through stretching after sunset when a Kiowa Warrior helicopter flew overhead scouting the area.

It banked hard.

Then turned directly toward us.

My brother looked at me.

"Do you think he saw us?"

I replied:

"We're like candlesticks out here. Of course he saw us."

Then suddenly the spotlight locked onto us.

It felt like we were fugitives on an episode of COPS.
My brother looked over.

"What do we do?"

The only thing I could think of was:

"Go somewhere public."

So we jumped into his 1986 white Chevrolet pickup truck and headed toward civilization on base.

The spotlight followed us the entire way.

Finally I pointed toward a Taco Bell.

"Maybe there."

We pulled into the parking lot while the spotlight lit up everything around us.

Moments later military police stormed the Taco Bell.

Five or six patrol cars.

We stood there in front of the truck while they searched inside.

Finally I yelled:

"Yoo-hoo! Over here!"

That got their attention.

An MP walked over and asked:
"What were you doing in that field?"

"We were doing karate."

He looked at me again.

"No really. What were you doing?"

"KARATE."

I explained that I used to teach and my brother wanted his first lesson while visiting me.

The MPs stared at both of us for a moment.

Then one finally pointed at Derek.
"You need to go home."

Then he pointed at me.

"You need to go back to the barracks."

I explained my brother had driven several hours to see me.

"Doesn't matter"

I finally asked if Derek could at least drive me back.

They agreed.

The ride back was quiet for about thirty seconds.

Then both of us started laughing.

The whole thing was completely absurd.

Meanwhile the hardship process kept getting more complicated.
The Army refused to ship my car from Alaska.

Whether it was retaliation or standard procedure, I honestly never figured out.

At this point my parents were about to lose their place to live and move into an unreliable camper.

Not a nice motorhome.

The kind of situation where homelessness feels dangerously close.

I knew I needed my car.

So I made the decision to drive it from Alaska myself.

A 2000 Dodge Neon with a cracked windshield from my DJ days.

The Army gave me one week.

Maps estimated the drive at sixty-eight hours.

I made it in seventy-two.

Winter conditions.

Over four thousand miles.

MapQuest became my best friend.

The Drive

I headed toward Tok and eventually Whitehorse, fascinated by the frozen-in-time feeling of those northern towns. One morning, I woke up to scenery so beautiful it looked like National Geographic. White snow. Blue-white roads. Heavy frozen trees. No camera. Just memory.

Another morning I woke up to temperatures around negative forty-one degrees.

I had plugged my car in overnight just to keep the engine alive. It still took fifteen minutes before heat finally came through the vents.

Eventually I made it into Saskatchewan and got pulled over for speeding. The Mountie returned with a ticket "by order of the Majesty of the Queen." I joked that I didn't know their queen, took the ticket, and kept driving.

Later that night the worst winter storm of the year rolled in.
At first the snow drifts appeared every thousand feet. Then more often.
Then suddenly everything disappeared into white.

My car hit deep snow and spun.

Ninety degrees.
Correction.
One-eighty.
Correction again.
Twice more.

Somehow I regained control without leaving the road. Then once stabilized, I parked slightly off to the side, got out and took a leak.

When I reached the border, the guard warned me.

"This is the worst storm of the year. If you try driving thirty miles to the next town, you could die in this storm."

I crossed anyway.

Later an officer found me near what looked like a ghost town and led me to a tiny upstairs apartment.

Green carpet.
Small room.
Peace.

The next morning he told me my plates came back to Hyatt Green.
"That's my brother," I said.

He told me to stay while they sorted it out.

I left instead.

At a gas stop near Chicago, I discovered both rear tires were showing steel belts.

Perfect.

I had to purchase two rear new tires.

Once on. I kept driving.

The Army denied my request for one extra day despite the storm and tire situation. I pushed through and made it back to Fort Campbell on time.

Pressure

When I returned, people seemed surprised I owned a newer car. The Neon was only a year old at the time.

By this point the hardship process had already changed how many people viewed me. Once word spreads that you are pursuing hardship, people start forming opinions whether they know your situation or not.
Still, I had to keep doing my job.

Night missions. Field exercises. Flying with pilots.

One night they purposely issued me defective night vision goggles.

One lens focused close.
The other far away.

Either it was to "get me used to flying" or retaliation for pursuing hardship.

Maybe both.

I nearly threw up during the flight.

Later they admitted they had done it intentionally.

Another night I was repeatedly climbing onto a seven-thousand-pound training block while a twelve-thousand-pound helicopter hovered overhead during cargo hook training.

The final attempt went wrong.

The helicopter drifted lower.

Closer. Closer. Too Close.

The moment I realized how close it was getting in the dark, I jumped.

That was one of the first times I fully realized:

I could die during training.

Around this same period, I became extremely focused on safety. One day during a ten-hour inspection, a calibration tool used on the helicopter blades fell from roughly sixteen feet off the aircraft.

By regulation, if that tool falls more than three feet, it must be recalibrated and inspected.

That was the standard.

A soldier who constantly threatened and mocked me demanded I hand him the tool without reporting the drop.

"This is my bird," he insisted.

He wanted the inspection completed his way.

I already had almost no trust from many people because of the hardship process.

By then I had assembled sixty-two pages of evidence and visited my attorney seventeen times.

A few months later I heard terrible news.

I hadn't been scheduled for a particular night training mission because of where I stood in the hardship process.

As crews returned afterward, everyone walked into the hangar in complete silence.

Then the word spread.

Two helicopters had collided during a night exercise.

No survivors.

That shook me deeply.

Some of the people from my unit never came home.

Others came back changed forever.

For me, it reinforced something I already knew.

The hardship wasn't theoretical anymore.

Life was moving fast.
And people were disappearing

Another situation escalated tensions further.
One evening before a mission, I carefully checked all my gear including my night vision goggles.

As I climbed into a Humvee, the strap snagged and the goggles fell off without me hearing it over all the engines running nearby.

During the drive I ended up having a cordial conversation with a young female lieutenant.

She knew about my hardship situation.

After talking for around twenty minutes and hearing more of what was happening, she looked at me and said:

"You know… you don't seem that bad."

People were already judging me.

That moment stayed with me.

Shortly after that conversation, I suddenly realized the NVGs were missing.

She had to radio it in.

The response was immediate.

Furious.

Eventually Sergeant Barks was dispatched to retrieve me.

He pulled up looking like an eighties action movie character.

Big mustache.

All muscle.

"You lost the goggles?"

"No. They fell off getting into the Humvee."

We drove back through rough terrain because he wanted to have a little fun along the way.

There they were.

Exactly where I said they would be.

Completely intact.

Did that redeem me?

Not even close.

To this day, before locking any door, I look at my keys in my hand.
I still think about it to this day.
That moment permanently changed me.

Eventually I reached the final stage of the hardship process.
The Colonel.

I don't remember his name, but I remember exactly how he carried himself.

Like Jack Nicholson in A Few Good Men.

"Green, you're not getting out."

I explained the evidence. The attorney meetings. The situation.

Didn't matter.

"You're not getting out. I'll see to that."

"Well sir… I have a Trump card."

"What is it?"

"You'll find out. I am going to pull it sir.
Then I'll be out in two weeks."

My Trump card was Congressman Don Young of Alaska. Don was in charge of the appropriations committee.

He reviewed my evidence and not long afterward my hardship discharge was approved.

Fully honorable.

September 10th, 2002.

One day before the anniversary of 9/11.

I was emotional when I got the news.

Partly because my military career was over.
Partly because I was finally getting my civilian freedom back.

I out-processed, turned in my gear, and left without saying goodbye to most people.

Some of those people I still talk to today.

I drove through Nashville and eventually arrived in Chattanooga.

A city I had already considered years earlier when my brother got married there in 2000.

I had already told myself back then:

"If my school doesn't make it in my hometown, I'll start over here."

I left the Army with uncertainty.

I was driving my silver 2000 Dodge Neon toward Chattanooga with no job lined up and no clear plan beyond rebuilding Green's Karate again someday.

My oldest brother let me stay with him for three months while I tried to figure life out.

I was grateful because at that point I really had nowhere else to go.

My brother Derek was building houses in places like Windstone and Council Fire.
Million-dollar homes.

I worked with him as a laborer making ten dollars an hour.
Honest work.
Carrying materials. Helping frame. Doing whatever needed to be done.

But I knew construction wasn't my long-term path.

So I picked up another job at Logan's as a server.
Oddly enough, I loved it.

If a conversation opened naturally, I would hand people my Green's Karate business card.

I was trying to build a dojo before I even had one.

Only six months after arriving in Chattanooga, Green's Karate entered the Downtown YMCA.

That moment changed everything.

At the time I didn't fully realize it yet…

but the foundation of the next twenty-plus years had just begun.

Underground

Green's Karate started two levels below ground beneath the Downtown YMCA.

The roof leaked from the women's shower area above us.

My office was in a stairwell.

Not beside it.

In it.

Teaching inside the YMCA changed me.
There were far more students with special needs than I had ever imagined.

I had taught some students in Alaska, but this was different.

The volume was bigger, the needs were bigger, and I was learning all over again too.

I had not taught much while serving in the Army.

Now I was suddenly back in an environment filled with students who learned differently.

Different personalities. Different processing. Different ways of understanding the world.
Some needed repetition. Some needed structure.
Some needed movement broken down differently.
Instead of becoming frustrated, I became fascinated.
Without realizing it, I had stopped simply teaching karate.

I had started studying people.
And eventually those observations would change everything.

Parents started noticing changes in their children.
Confidence. Focus. Discipline. Social growth.
Kids who struggled in other environments sometimes started thriving inside class.

That caught my attention immediately.

Some students needed more repetition.
Some needed movement broken down differently.
Some needed structure.
Some needed calmer instruction.

Others needed encouragement at exactly the right moment.

The more I taught, the more fascinated I became.
The students who impacted me the most were often the students who needed the most patience.

Those students changed me.
They forced me to slow down.

Observe more.
Adapt more.
Think differently.

I stopped asking:

"How do I teach karate?"

And started asking:

"How does this person learn?"

That question changed everything.

At the time, I thought I was rebuilding Green's Karate.

Green's Karate was rebuilding me.

The more students I taught, the more patterns I started noticing.
Body language. Processing speed. Confidence shifts. Timing.
Positioning.
Tiny details most people probably never saw started standing out everywhere.

Some students could hear the instructions perfectly but still struggled to execute them.

Others needed to see it. Others needed to feel it.
Others needed repetition.

The same lesson did not work the same way for everyone.

That fascinated me.

Without realizing it, I had started moving away from one-size-fits-all teaching.

Traditional martial arts often expects students to adapt to the instructor.

I started adapting instruction to the student.

That changed everything.

The more I observed, the more obsessed I became with understanding why.
Why visual structure helped.
Why rhythm mattered.
Why encouragement worked differently depending on the person.
Why some students flourished once they simply understood.

At the time, I thought I was teaching karate.

Looking back now…

I was beginning to engineer instruction.

Around this same period, one student quietly started changing everything.

Brandon Earnshaw.

At first, he was simply another student training inside Green's Karate.

Nobody knew history was approaching.

Including me.

At the time, martial arts viewed autism very differently.
Expectations were lower.
Opportunities were smaller.

And in many cases, students were separated before they ever had the chance to show what they could do.

I was starting to see something different.

Potential.

I was not interested in labels.

I wanted to understand how people learned.

How they processed information.

How they performed under pressure.

And Brandon kept proving people wrong.
Over and over again.

He trained hard.
Really hard.

Not because the journey was easy.

Because he refused to quit.

Eventually that effort carried him somewhere nobody had gone before.

Neither of us knew it yet.

But history was already moving.

GREEN'S
KARATE
KICKBOXIN

GREEN'S
KARATE
KICKBOXIN
10 20 '04

The First Time History Was Made

2006, Green's Karate was finally starting to gain real traction in Chattanooga.

Not overnight.
Not through luck.

Through years of rebuilding, adapting, surviving, and constantly refining how I taught.

The school programs were growing.
The YMCA programs were growing.
The competition team was growing.

And quietly…

history was approaching.

What makes this story even crazier is where all of it was happening. Green's Karate operated two levels underground beneath the Downtown YMCA.

There were classes eventually days a week. In the beginning it was only 4 and then we expanded to six days a week.

Students eventually started asking about competing and in 2005 we went to only one tournament. In 2006, we hit the tournament circuit for experience.

history was quietly forming.

That year I brought six competitors to the U.S. National Championships.

Including two father-and-son teams.
Both fathers were Marines.

That mattered to me because there is something different about fathers stepping onto the competition floor beside their children.

The pressure becomes shared.

The experience becomes shared.

One of the sons was still only a green belt.
Fifth kyu.
Intermediate division.

Because of low numbers, he was bumped into the advanced division against brown and black belts.

Around twenty-five competitors.

Most people probably assumed he would get overwhelmed.
He didn't.
He fought his way to fourth and fifth place in kata and kumite.

As a green belt. 1st time at Nationals, ever.

Against advanced competitors.

That performance turned heads.

His father won gold in kumite and silver in kata.
The other Marine father won bronze in kumite.

The youngest competitor was only five years old and still fought his way to two fourth-place finishes. He is the son of the marine that won bronze.

Everybody left learning something.

About pressure.
About themselves.

Then there was Brandon.

At first we were too busy training to realize what was happening.
Competing. Traveling. Preparing. Working.

We were simply doing what we always did.
Then Brandon's mother started sending emails out sharing the story two weeks before Nationals

Local reporter Rick Nyman from WDEF picked it up first.

After that, everything started moving quickly.

Then CNN called.

They met us at Nationals in Fort Lauderdale and followed us for three days. The preparation, competition, interviews, pressure and emotion.

That was when it finally hit me.

Brandon had become the "first athlete with autism to compete in the non-handicap division at U.S. Karate Nationals."

History had happened quietly.

While we were busy doing the work.

And suddenly something that started two levels underground in Chattanooga was reaching far beyond those walls.

CNN's story traveled worldwide.

Then the local cameras came.
Then the local interviews came.

And the story growing beneath those floors started reaching the world.
The story did more than bring attention to Brandon.

I started THE conversation.

People began realizing something many had never considered before.
People with autism could do martial arts.

They could compete.
They could thrive.

The CNN story was not the peak.

It was the beginning.

Because more breakthroughs were coming.
More athletes were coming.
More impossible moments were coming.

But 2006 was the first time the outside world truly saw what Green's Karate was becoming.
Not just a martial arts school.

A place where people others underestimated could discover what they were capable of.

Thinking about it, it feels surreal. At the time, we were simply doing the work.

History Again

At first, I thought Brandon was one extraordinary story.

One breakthrough.
One impossible moment.

Then, history happened again.

In 2007, another student with autism joined the Green's Karate competition team.

Alex Davidson.

What surprised me was the speed.

Brandon had taken around two and a half years to develop into a national-level competitor.

In 2006 to 2007, Alex was progressing in less than half that time.

That mattered.

Because it meant the methods themselves were evolving.

Three years later, another student quietly kept building too.

Katie Dietsche.

Different student.
Different journey.

Same lesson.

Potential.

By this point, Green's Karate was growing from multiple directions at once. The YMCA remained the home base.

At the same time I was teaching in after-school programs throughout Chattanooga.

Early on, I picked up one of the most exclusive private schools in the city and stayed there thirteen years.

I also taught at Montessori for thirteen years.

Classes. Schools.
YMCA programs.
Competition teams.

Everything was happening simultaneously.

I was building Green's Karate outwardly multiplying into various directions.

Then life shifted again.

In 2007, the Downtown YMCA announced an eight-million-dollar renovation project.

I had to move.

Again.

Fortunately, the Eastgate YMCA was still running.

So while one chapter was ending, another location helped keep momentum alive.

But the moves were not over yet.

Not even close.

Research

By late 2009, another unexpected chapter had opened.
From October through late January of 2010, I participated in research through LUDIC, the Lee University Development Inclusion Classroom.

Five students.
Four boys. One girl.

All with severe autism. Non verbal.

16 sessions for 30 minutes each.

The project operated under **I**nstitutional **R**eview **B**oard approval. Human subjects research.

I had already developed a deep understanding movement, learning patterns, and how people processed information.

The research accelerated that understanding.
It forced me to observe differently.
To think differently. To adapt differently.

At the time, I was simply trying to help.

While conducting research, I realize I was learning again.

The timing was surreal.

While the research was happening. Green's Karate was still running.
The schools were still running. Competition was still running.

Life never slowed down.

Then MLK weekend arrived.

Three days of rebuilding the dojo.

And everything moved again.

Rebuilding Again

The gym I was leasing from was closing in 10 days.
I called the EastGate YMCA.
Got the dreaded, "The number you have called has been disconnected"

10 days notice. I had to find a dojo for the next decade.
I went up and down the roads nearest my soon to be closed location.

I found it .25 miles away.
30 people helped with 10 pickups, a jeep with a trailer and a box truck.

1 hour and 5 minutes move time.

And...

MLK weekend had arrived.

Three days to build a dojo.
That was all I had.
The dojo came apart.
Then went back together again.

Pads. Equipment. Offices. Storage.

Everything moved.

Students kept training.

The school was still running.

Competition was still moving forward.

Life never slowed down.

I had just finished research.

History was already starting to build.

And somehow, in the middle of all of it, Green's Karate kept growing.

History Again

2010, history happened again.

Katie Dietsche became the first girl with autism to qualify and compete in the non-handicap division.

History did not arrive all at once. In 2010, Katie Dietsche became the first girl with autism to qualify and compete in the non-handicap division, while Ryan Rogers had already entered the picture in 2009 asking about USA Karate competition.

In January 2012, Katie Whipple started training.

Seven months later, Katie Whipple stood at Nationals and won gold and silver.

All three trained together in that little dojo. We called them "The Two Katies" and Ryan.

At the time they were just students.

Also, I was not thinking about history. I was thinking about teaching, adapting, and helping.

I knew the Karate Wise methods were already coming together, and that little dojo became the proving ground for what was coming next.

Their timelines were converging.

That dojo had expanded from 800 to 1,200 square feet with one bathroom in the waiting area and one in the dojo. The training floor itself was only about 700 square feet, yet thirteen historical moments came out of that space:

8 Times

2012 arrived.
Katie Whipple had only trained for seven months.
Ryan Rogers had been building quietly since 2009.

The little dojo kept moving. The methods kept evolving.
And then Nationals happened.

In 2012 alone, Green's Karate students made U.S. karate history eight separate times.

Two of those accomplishments came through Katie Whipple and were fully verified at the time. Ryan Rogers would not receive his autism diagnosis until late 2013, after he had already made U.S. karate history six times himself.

By the end of 2012, *eight historic milestones had already occurred.
At that point, I stopped viewing the breakthroughs as coincidences.
(*See Reflection for all historical information.)

Something was happening. I just did not fully understand it yet.

Katie Whipple was blind.

At the time she was simply another student walking into the dojo.

Seven months later she stood on the National stage and won gold and silver.

Katie Whipple did not train the way most people expected.

I had already been studying movement, learning patterns, and how people processed information.

Without realizing it, Karate Wise methods were already starting to emerge. Seven months later those methods stood on the National stage.

Nationals became convergence.

The breakthroughs were not happening in isolation anymore.

Ryan was there. Katie Whipple was there.
The little dojo was there.

The timelines that had started years apart were now standing on the same floor.

At the time, they were simply students.

Now, I realize they were becoming something more.

2013 Nationals arrived.

History happened again.

Ryan's story was still unfolding.

Ryan had earned a black belt before he ever began training with me. When he joined Green's Karate, he chose to start over from the beginning, which is why his early national accomplishments came while competing in Novice divisions.

He had entered the picture in 2009 asking about USA Karate competition.

By 2012 he was still building.
In 2012, Ryan made U.S. Karate history four times.

One for being the first person with autism to medal in able bodied divisions. Secondly, for winning silver in kata in the novice 18-34 year old and thirdly, bronze in the 18-34 year old kumite division in 2012. Finally, Ryan took the officials exam passed it and became the first person with autism to become a USANKF National Judge for kata and Judge for kumite.

In 2013, Ryan made history again, this time in intermediate kumite for ages 18-34.

Later that same year or 2013 came the autism diagnosis.

The diagnosis did not explain what Ryan could do.
It explained what he already overcome.

2015 arrived.

Ryan entered five divisions.

He came home with two gold medals.

That same year he began officiating.

History happened again.

Ryan became the first person with autism (shared) to compete in the advanced 18-34 kata and as well as the 18-34 kumite division as well.

Nothing

By 2015, Nationals had become something very different for me.
I was no longer just walking in as a coach trying to survive the experience.
I was carrying multiple responsibilities at once.

Coach. Instructor. Mentor. Official.

That year, I had to leave the night before and because I was scheduled to test for my next referee certification. I mistakenly miscalculated the trip and when we needed to leave.

The kata portion was intense.

You had to physically perform a kata in front of a panel of three WKF officials.

You had to perform a kata not even from your own style.

A different style entirely.

I was exhausted before I even walked in.

I had driven from Chattanooga to Fort Lauderdale, slept maybe an hour in the car, and went straight into testing.

There was also a one-hundred-question written exam. 30 seconds per question and you cannot go back.
Fifty kata.
Fifty kumite.

This was not casual officiating anymore.

My number was seven.

I walked behind the large closed door and performed Rohai.

No warmup. No practice. Cold.

When I finished, the center official said,

"I don't have any questions."

He turned to the official to the right of him, looked and said,

"Do you have any questions?"

"No. I don't have any questions."

Then the other.

"No I do not have any questions."

"Good job, Mr. Green."

I bowed and walked out.

The second the door closed behind me, I fist-pumped the air like a little kid. YESSS!

Then I walked back into the waiting room.
Everyone asked the same question.

"What did they ask you?"
I smiled.

"Nothing."

In January of 2016, I was added to the Athletes with Disabilities Committee for USA Karate.

At the time the committee was small. It still is today.

The head coach Jeffery Kohn, Tokey Hill, Sasha Gerritson and myself serve on this committee.

Around this same time another season was ending.
One of the schools I had taught at for years decided to move in a different direction.

The principal told me the parents loved our program and there had never been complaints in thirteen years.

But they needed to do what they felt was best.

My last month was May of 2016.

Two months later, in July, Ryan made the United States Olympic Karate Team (Para)

One door closed.
Another opened.

Life kept teaching me the same lesson.

Nothing lasts forever. Not the hard seasons.
Not the good seasons.

Everything changes.

The key is learning when it is time to move forward.

Photo Credit: Dave McMahan

The U.S. Karate Team

July of 2016 arrived.

Ryan Rogers made the U.S. Karate Team.

He became the first athlete with autism on the U.S. Team.

Seven years eariler he had simply asked if he could compete.

Now he was representing the United States.

I sat with that for a while.

Not because it was history.

Because I remember where he started.

One student, one question, one opportunity.

And now the door had opened that had never opened before.

My last month at the school had been May of 2016..

Two months later Ryan made the team.

One chapter had ended.

Another had begun.

Seven hundred square feet.

The Two Katies.

Ryan.

For a little dojo tucked away in Chattanooga, that wasn't suppose to happend.

But it did.

In 2013 I published my first book. A children's book.

Finding Karate.

When I arrived in Chattanooga in 2002, I visited many of the local schools and realized something surprising.

Even some places using the word karate were not actually teaching Japanese karate.

At first, I thought that would make things easier.

I thought people looking for karate would eventually find me.

Ten years later I realized something else.

The message was not reaching people.

So I wrote a children's book.

The story followed a boy named Bucky Longbottom from River City. He visited real karate schools, real taekwondo schools, and real kung fu schools.

Then he found one advertising karate that was not teaching it.

The book was not written to criticize.

It was written to educate.

If the adults were not listening, maybe the kids would.

There was another reason too.

I had never published a book before.

Finding Karate taught me the process.

Later, when it came time to publish Karate Wise, I had already walked that road once.

Karate Wise

While Finding Karate was being written, another project had already begun.

Karate Wise.

I had started working on it in 2008. I thought at the time that nobody else was doing what I was doing. I felt like I needed to make something that would be easy to follow that would help teachers and parents learn how to teach their own child karate.

At the time I had no idea it would take ten years.
The photo shoots ran from 2011 through 2014.

80% of the students in Karate Wise are neuro-divergent.

Thousands of images. Teaching layers, structure and assembly.
The project fought me. Laying out a book with hundreds of photos does workout the way you think it would. I know exactly what to do now.

Layout. Organization. Flow

How to explain what I was doing in a way others could teach.

It would not finally be completed until 2018.

Finding Karate explained what karate was.

Karate Wise teaches you how.

Karate Wise. OSS!!!

Austria

October of 2016 arrived.

Ryan Rogers stood on the floor at the World Karate Championships in Linz, Austria.

The student who had once asked about competition in 2009 was now standing on the world stage seven years later.

Karate had entered it's Olympic era. 2016-2021

For many of us, this was the moment we had waited for.

The Opening Ceremonies felt magical because the dream had finally become real.

You could feel it in the arena.

The official theme song of the World Championships was,"We Are Karate." It premiered during the Opening Ceremonies.

The celebration was bigger than the tournament itself.

The world was celebrating karate's arrival to the Olympics.

Ryan became the first American with autism to compete at the World Karate Championships.

He finished 6th in the world out of 24 competitors.

History happened again. Soldotna. Chattanooga.
Seven hundred square feet. Then
Austria.

And what none of us knew then was that this Olympic chapter would only last one cycle.

Karate had finally arrived.
And almost as quickly, it would be gone again.

Joel

2016 brought another student into the dojo.

His name is Joel Westbrook.

Nicknamed "Powerhouse"

At the time he was simply another student coming through the door.

Knowing Joel now, I had no idea who or what was coming.

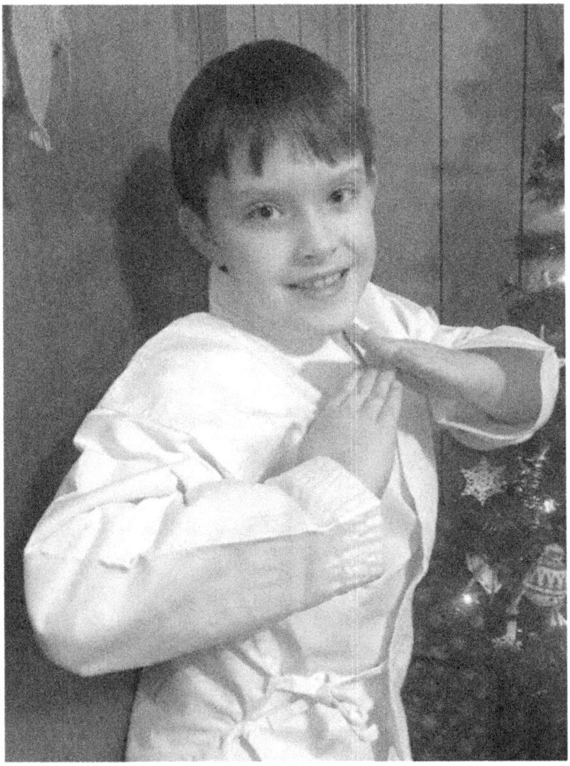

Curacao

2017 brought us to Curacao for the PKF International Karate Championships.

Ryan competed in kata representing the United States while my wife and I stepped onto our first island together.

The beauty was beyond imagination, and for the first time in my life I stepped into water I had dreamed about since childhood.

My wife wanted elegance.

I wanted my feet in the ocean.

It felt like Christmas morning.

Ryan finished with the silver medal.

Looking back now, I still believe gold was there.

Curacao gave me memories beyond the medal.

Gold

While life was getting harder at home, the dojo kept moving forward.

Ryan Rogers and Joel Westbrook both competed.

Both won gold.

Joel earned his first National championship in the wheelchair division.

Another student was building his own story.

Mac.

In 2017, a local businessman helped his mother with the cost of attending the 2017 USANKF Karate National Championships.

When Mac stepped onto the floor, he made the opportunity count.

National Champion

Then he stepped into the non-handicap divisions and gave everything he had.

He reminded me of Brandon a decade eariler.

That act of kindness mattered from the businessman because it fostered a dream for a kid.

Year later Mac attended Tennessee Tech.

Straight A's.

Proof that one moment of help can change a life.

The dojo kept teaching me the same lesson.

People grow. People rise.

Sometimes all they need is an opportunity.

Very Severe Aplastic Anemia

A few months earlier, my wife and I had been sitting on the beach in Curacao.

For a brief moment life felt calm.

We were drinking tropical drinks, enjoying the island, and simply being together.

While we were there, we noticed something strange.

Michelle kept bruising easily.

At first it did not seem like a huge deal.
Just random bruises.

A couple months later everything changed.

Michelle was diagnosed with very severe aplastic anemia.

She could not make blood.
Life changed overnight.

Because she is allergic to ALL antibiotics, her survival odds became even lower.

Eventually she underwent equine ATG therapy where her immune system was essentially wiped out and rebooted.

At one point her platelets dropped to around six thousand.
The hospital eventually told her she could not go home at twelve-thousand platelets.

What followed was years of hospital visits.
Emergency situations. Bloodwork. Fear. Survival.
Ten days here. Five days there.
Over a hundred visits over the years.

And meanwhile life kept moving.

Ryan kept competing.

Joel had entered the dojo.

Karate Wise was still being built quietly in the background.

The dojo still had to operate.

That is what made 2017 feel surreal.

One side of my life was growing into new possibilities.

The other side felt like it was collapsing in real time.

I kept teaching. I kept building. I kept moving.

Because stopping was not an option.

Can't Hurt Me

In January of 2018, I attended a Pruvit event and listened to David Goggins speak for around two hours.

He mentioned a book he was working on titled, "Can't Hurt Me."

Listening to him, something clicked. He had no idea Karate Wise existed, but I remember thinking the same thing about my own project: I have to finish this once and for all.

Karate Wise had started in 2008.

It survived computer crashes, layout battles, thousands of photos, rewrites, organization problems, and life itself.

Ten years.

In April of 2018, it was finally finished.

The timing felt strange.

Just as one decade-long project ended, another chapter of survival was beginning

New Roads

When I came back from Reno, reality was waiting.
Nationals were over. The trip was over.
But survival was just beginning.

I pulled into Walmart with around one hundred twenty-five dollars left to my name.

That was it.

I walked inside and bought seat covers for the back seats of my new 2018 Hyundai Elantra Value Edition. Then I went back outside, opened the doors, and installed them right there in the parking lot while the sun was going down.

I remember standing there looking at the car.

Karate Wise had finally been released after almost ten years of work.

Ryan and Joel had just competed at Nationals.

My wife was still recovering.

And now I was about to become an Uber driver.

I said a small prayer.

Turned the app on.
And waited.

The first passenger I ever picked up was a hairstylist who smelled like weed.
I remember thinking:

"Great. This is how the car gets broken in."

At the time, I had no idea what was beginning.

That little Hyundai would eventually carry athletes, books, passengers, food deliveries, television appearances, and more than ten thousand trips.

It would carry survival.

That parking lot feels bigger than it did then.

Because sometimes life does not announce the start of a new chapter.

Sometimes it begins quietly.

One prayer. One car. One app.

And about one hundred twenty-five dollars.

Spain

Later in 2018, Ryan Rogers made the U.S. Karate Team again and we traveled to Madrid, Spain for the World Championships. Michelle was still recovering and needed a wheelchair in the airport because she was still weak, which made the trip emotional considering everything we had already survived. At the same time, Ryan was now representing the United States internationally. Looking around Madrid, it hit me again how improbable that journey really was.

Outside competition, we explored museums together in Madrid. Walking through history while carrying our own history felt strangely grounding. Hospitals, uncertainty, survival, and fear had consumed so much of life that simply slowing down and taking things in mattered. Sometimes you need moments like that to remember life is still happening around you. Training never stopped. At one point Ryan practiced underground in a parking garage surrounded by concrete pillars and echoes. No spotlight. No crowd. Just work. Looking back, that image perfectly represented our journey: hidden effort before visible results.

After a day in Madrid, Michelle and I spent about three days in Barcelona. The city felt artistic, alive, and different from Madrid somehow. More importantly, after years of medical battles, we finally had a moment to breathe. Not forever. Just enough. We came back to the karate world Championships and I trained my athlete some more before the event.

One of my favorite memories came from a reaction-time challenge at the event. Michelle walked herself up there and threw a backfist despite everything she had been through. She ended up recording the second-fastest reaction time there, beating world-level athletes decades younger than her. After surviving aplastic anemia, that moment said everything about who she was.

Ryan competed vwell in Madrid but did not medal Spain had three competitors in the division and finished first, second, and third out of the twenty-nine athletes entered. Sometimes it is built in showing up, learning, and coming back stronger.

Things Were Working Again

Strangely enough, around this time, things finally started improving again.

The dojo was growing. Classes were filling.
Students were coming in.

After years of pressure, hospitals, uncertainty, and survival, it finally felt like the work was starting to pay off.

For a moment, life felt like it was coming together.

The athletes were succeeding.

Karate Wise was finished.

Uber was helping hold things together financially.

And the dojo was moving forward again.

I remember thinking:

"Okay… maybe we made it."

We had no idea what was coming next.

Panama

In May of 2019, Ryan Rogers represented the United States again at the international championships in Panama.

Ryan had already made the U.S. Karate Team in 2018, which led to Spain later that year and now Panama.

By this point, international competition had become part of our lives.

Training. Travel. Preparation. Pressure.

And Ryan kept answering the call.

In Panama, Ryan put down what I still believe was a gold-medal level performance.

But international competition can become complicated.

Rules. Systems. Classification. Interpretation.

Sometimes the outcome is not only about the performance itself.
Ryan ultimately returned with bronze.

Looking back, I still have mixed emotions about it.

Because as a coach, you see the work.

You see the preparation. You see the performance.
And sometimes you quietly believe the result should have been different.

But that is part of sports too.

You learn. You adapt. You keep moving forward.
And meanwhile, back home, something else was happening.

The dojo was filling up again.

Fifteen to eighteen students packed into around seven hundred square feet.

For the first time in years, we were successful again.

And I realized:

We had officially outgrown the building.

Ringgold Road

By late 2019, I knew the dojo had outgrown the building.
We were successful again.

The athletes were succeeding.

Classes were full.

Sometimes fifteen to eighteen students were packed into around seven hundred square feet.

I had been there almost ten years.

It was time. I was planning for double the rent for double the space. What I got was double the rent for four times the space or eight times in volume.

People often ask, where is your studio? I half jokingly say, I have a mansion.

At first, I drove up and down Hixson Pike looking where my dojo currrently was.
Nothing felt right.

Eventually I found myself on Ringgold Road zigzagging through parking lots and looking at buildings.

Then I saw it.

I walked up to the glass and looked inside.

The back wall looked far away.

I remember thinking:

"Wow."

Something immediately felt different.

During negotiations I noticed there was no back door.

I called the realtor.

"Hey… there's no back door."

"There's no back door?"

"Nope. But I think we should put one in."

Eventually double doors were added.

The vision slowly started becoming real.

Michelle was scared.

I asked:

"Are you scared?"

She said:

"Yes."

I said:

"I'm not."

She asked why.
I told her:

"Because I talked to God."

"What is God telling you?"

"Go."
"Go."
"Go."

There were four choices.

Stay. Move earlier. Move later.
Or move exactly when I did.
Staying would not work.
The dojo was too small.

Moving earlier runs into COVID.

Moving later misses the timing completely and the opportunity changes.

The only answer was risk.

And around that time something else hit me.

Twenty years earlier, around 2000, I had already experienced the crash.

The rebuilding.
The uncertainty.

Standing there preparing to take the biggest risk of my career, I realized something:

2000 had been preparing me for 2020.

I just did not know it yet.

Back then life happened to me.

Now I was choosing the risk.

I remember standing inside the building looking around.
White walls. Huge open space. Twenty-five-foot ceilings.
Most people probably saw an empty building.
I saw possibility. I had MADE IT.

At least that is what I thought.

After everything…
Alaska. The crash. The rebuilding. Opening the dojo. The struggles.

Michelle's illness.

Uber.

The survival.

I thought we had finally arrived.

This place felt enormous.

It still feels like a mansion of a dojo.

But back then, I had no idea what was waiting less than two weeks ahead.

We had only been in the building about two weeks.

The world shut down.

Stories From The Driver's Seat

The idea of writing a book about my passengers came after appearing on This N That in July of 2018 with one of my Uber passengers within two weeks of driving for Rideshare.

Driving had introduced me to thousands of people, stories, and moments, so I started saving them.

I missed some of the earliest rides, but by around day eleven I began documenting everything and later went back trying to reconstruct what I could.

What people do not realize is that I wrote that book while simultaneously driving Uber and Lyft, growing the dojo, traveling for karate, moving locations, and simply trying to survive.

It took around eighteen months to write my third book.

Not because the book was difficult.

Because life was.

The first book signing was supposed to happen in February.
Then it snowed.

So I canceled it and moved it.
The new date became:

March 14th, 2020.

Ta da.

After Saturday classes, I still went.

The signing happened.

I remember sitting there trying to sell a travel book while the world was

beginning to panic.
People were frantic. Uncertain. Focused on survival.

I sold one copy.
To a police officer from Georgia.

Three weeks before the world shut down, I was selling them out of my car like hotcakes. I truly thought that the book signing was going to go bonkers but instead people went bonkers.

That detail still makes me laugh.

The world was beginning to shut down.
Travel was collapsing.

I had just moved into the biggest dojo of my life.

And somehow a Georgia cop walked away with my travel book.

Truth is stranger than fiction. Sometimes.

First the snow. Then the reschedule. Then history.

Stories From the Driver's Seat had finally arrived.

And the world stopped traveling. And everything got buried.

Survival Mode

When the world shut down, I pivoted immediately. Just three food deliveries before, and now I was full-on into Uber Eats, every night, every order. The money started coming in faster than I expected. And the owners of the building, just as the world shut down, told me: "Don't worry about rent right now, you just got here. We'll figure it out." I told them I was so grateful, and I meant it.

But when food deliveries pay slowed down by May, I knew I had to turn back to the dojo.

The Small Business Administration hadn't come through yet, but by July, when the SBA funds arrived, I reinvested every bit into the dojo. I had been fighting to survive, trying to stay above water, and after weeks of confusion, I reached out again. This time to Uber, explaining I'd done everything right, but I was stuck. Someone said, "Contact your congressman." And I did.

Within days, Uber called, and they sent me $7,800. I told the building owner, and he said, "Good, we wanted to work with you." And finally, after all that fighting, I kept going.

If you look at my 2020 timeline, from January to December, it was a huge arc. Early on, business was strong, but by mid-year, everything collapsed.

And I want to be clear: I didn't just drive in Chattanooga; I drove to Nashville.

From 2018 until the unfortunate shutdown of the world, I was making about $60 an hour there, far more than in Chattanooga, where I'd only see $20 to $25. People told me I wasn't doing it right, but Nashville was where I thrived. And something else: all the New Yorkers I met in my car...100% of them...were kind.

When I drove for Uber and Lyft, it was never my first choice; it was when student numbers fell short. I ran projections, percentages, and timelines—but I couldn't count chickens before they hatched. I was let down so often by people who said one thing and did another, so I took the wheel myself.

I drove to Nashville, two hours each way because before the world shut down,

I was making $60 an hour there, while Chattanooga paid $20 or $25. And there was something else, every New Yorker I met in my car, all of them, without fail, were kind. I get why they seem tough in New York,they have to be, but man, if I ever went to war, I'd stand next to a New Yorker in a heartbeat.

And after 2020, I saw it: kids came in so much heavier, especially the girls, with that weight of isolation.

But by 2021, some students returned, though it didn't last as long as I hoped.

People say it's just the economy,
I do not think that is all of it.

Children changed.

When the world shut down, isolation increased, electronic devices increased. Depression increased.

And I saw it.

Especially in the girls.

Some students walked into the dojo carrying a weight that had not been there before.

Karate became more than training again.

It became restoration.

I built this dojo so I would not have to chase after-school programs anymore.

Because when you teach inside a child's environment, it is different.

They are home.

But when they walk into the dojo, they enter your environment.

The focus, expectation and effort changes.

People ask why karate matters.

Here is my answer:

Kids need challenge, failure, effort, community, and kids need to struggle at something and discover they can overcome it.

That is what karate gave me.

And that is what I wanted to give back.

Harvard 2012 Electronic devices study ages 10 and under should not be on any device for more than 2 hours per day. It decreases gray matter in the brain. Gray matter is responsible for processing information.

Guess what?

Studies have recently shown that karate adds the gray matter back.

Kids need a place where they take it karate seriously.

And I'm here for that.

No matter what.

Building the Dream

For three months, I taught virtually with a full setup built around three televisions while simultaneously preparing the new dojo. Then I signed off and spent the final thirty days building because it was time.

The SBA funds came in, and I went to work. Two hundred mats shipped from China to the East Coast, so I rented a U-Haul, made another road trip, and brought them home.

I installed seven six-foot mirrors, painted the entire dojo with a scissor lift, and somehow never hit a wall or anything else.

Why?

Because I can drive.

Less than ninety days earlier, the building had been empty.

Now it was becoming a dojo.

The warehouse feeling was disappearing.
The vision was finally becoming real.

Then came the grand opening.

Ribbon cutting.

Radio station.
People walking through the doors.

For a moment, it felt like maybe we had outrun it.

And it was done right down to the wire.

Why? Why not?

This is my story. And that is exactly how it happened.

Third Act of Congress

Food delivery eventually slowed down.

The money was not the same anymore.

So I tried to do what the system wanted.

Find a job.

The problem was I had not looked for a job in over twenty years.

Weeks went by. Nothing.
Everything was shut down.

Then someone told me:

"You should contact your congressman."

I had already lived this story twice before.

The Army. Then again.

Now here it was a third time.
Two days later, I got the call.

Around $7,800 was coming.

I called the building owners.

I told them I could start paying again.

And they told me something I will never forget:

"You're the kind of person we want to work with."

That mattered.

If you looked at my income graph for 2020, it looked like a giant "U."
January started high.

Then it dropped.

Lower. Lower.

Until around July.

Then slowly…
very slowly…

it started climbing again toward the end of the year.

November. December.
Hope.

A lot of businesses closed when the world shut down.

I understood why.

But I survived because I had learned something:

Never rely on one thing.

Teaching. Uber. Lyft. Food delivery. Books.

Whatever it took.

That became the strategy.

Around December 26th through the 30th,

I drove to Chicago trying to make food delivery money because Nashville had stopped paying as well.

I thought maybe a bigger city would help.

It didn't.

I basically broke even.

Looking back, it was a bad move financially.

But when I got home, I did what I always did.

I kept teaching.
I kept driving.

That was it.

Nonstop.

The Invisible Enemy

We had been careful.

Really careful.

But you cannot protect someone everywhere they go.

A family member attended a large gathering, became sick, and unknowingly passed the virus to Michelle.
Because of her medical history, we already knew this was dangerous.

Timing mattered. Everything mattered.

The hospital told us we needed to go to the main hospital.
I drove her myself.

Crossing the bridge, a tear rolled down my face.
Michelle looked at me and said:

"You better stop crying right now. I'm going to make it."

She spent nine days in the hospital.
I could not see her for the first six.

When I finally got in, she was on oxygen.

Still fighting.
She came home.
But the fight was not over.
She remained on oxygen for 3 months.

And once again…

we survived.

The Olympics

The Olympics finally happened in 2021.

Karate had never been in the Olympics before.

Japan, being the host country, wanted to showcase sports tied to its culture and identity. Baseball, softball, surfing, skateboarding and naturally, karate all became part of the conversation.

Karate was approved for the Tokyo Olympics in 2016 and officially announced shortly after. For the first time ever, karate would be on the Olympic stage.

You might wonder, Wait… I thought karate was already in the Olympics.

No. That would be Tae Kwon Do.

Tae Kwon Do appeared as a demonstration sport in Seoul, Korea in 1988 before becoming a full Olympic sport in 2000. Judo had already been an

Olympic sport since 1964.

I actually felt bad for break dancing.

Both karate and break dancing had moments that brought attention for reasons outside the sport itself. For karate, many people still remember the final kumite match. I am not even going to say who was fighting because for those that follow karate… they already know.

And for break dancing, I think most people can see what happened there too.

Sometimes when a sport becomes Olympic, it risks losing part of its roots.

The next time karate, break dancing, or any developing sport gets its opportunity, I hope they stay true to what made them special in the first place because greatness still comes from practice, talent and desire.

I also think there is room one day for something bigger.

Imagine an Olympic martial arts category with individual disciplines and divisions beneath it:

Karate | Kung Fu | Tae Kwon Do
Judo | Japanese Jujutsu | Muay Thai | Brazilian Jiu-Jitsu
Different systems. Different cultures. Different histories.

One stage.

Maybe someday the world gets to see all of them together.

The Rise of Joel Westbrook

The day the world shut down changed a lot of things. Competitions disappeared. The world slowed down. But while much of the world stood still, Joel kept building.

Year after year he returned stronger. More control. More confidence. More experience. Every season added another layer until the athlete people saw was no longer the athlete they remembered.

Joel did not rise all at once. He rose gradually. Quietly. Repetition after repetition, competition after competition, year after year.

What many people do not see is the work between the medals. The training. The failures. The adjustments. The decision to come back again and again. One season became another. Gold medals kept stacking. Progress kept building. Before long Joel was not just winning, he was becoming part of history.

He became the first male wheelchair athlete on the U.S. Karate Team. Not because someone opened the door for him, but because he kept pushing until the door moved.

Every year he seemed to return stronger than the year before.
More polished. More dangerous. More prepared.

The ashes of the world shutting down did not stop him. They became the ground he rose from.

People see the medals now. I see the journey. The repetitions. The long road that carried him there.

Powerhouse was not given to Joel. He earned it over time. One season at a time. One challenge at a time. One rise after another.

That is why his story matters. It reminds us that growth is rarely explosive. Sometimes it looks like quietly becoming stronger every year until one day the world finally notices.

While Joel kept rising season after season, something else was happening. I was building again. Not just classes or tournaments. Systems. Websites. Apps. Ideas that had been waiting for years.

For years survival had taken priority. Keep the dojo alive. Keep teaching. Keep moving. Keep going.

Then something changed. The builder came back. Ideas that had lived quietly for years suddenly began moving again.

In December of 2025, I began rebuilding Green's Karate online. By late January, the website was finished and growing. Then came the apps, another website, and finally the work of assembling Improbable itself.

The dojo had always been more than four walls and mats.

For the first time in a long time, I was not just suriving.

I was building again.

Years earlier I had spent eleven days as an extra on the movie 42. I never found myself in the film and eventually forgot all about it.

Then years later Joel reached his forty-second gold medal.
Suddenly the memory came back.

I laughed when I realized it. All those years later and somehow the number had returned again.

Life had done that more than once. Moments disappear for years, then suddenly return carrying new meaning.

Maybe that is part of getting older. You begin looking backward and realize life had been weaving things together all along.

Joked and wondered what would happen when I eventually reached the

movie 300.

Maybe nothing.
Maybe everything.

I have always liked Richard Petty. Longevity. Consistency. Showing up again and again.

Maybe that is what life really is. Not one great moment. Not one victory.

Just continuing.

Keep teaching. Keep helping. Keep building. Keep going.

Joel with his bronze medal he won in Rio May 2026. This was our 21st time making history thanks to our students.

From the summer of 2025 until Egypt I worked Taggr jobs. A parking enforcement company thats nation-wide.
In six months, I issued over six thousand parking tickets.

Second place nationwide had around forty-two hundred.

I was paid five dollars a ticket.
The work mattered.

It helped keep everything moving.

The tickets came from all eighteen lots across Chattanooga.

Month after month I averaged around a thousand tickets.

Sometimes more.
Sometimes less.

At the same time I was cleaning Airbnbs.

Laundry running.
Run to the lot.
Tag cars.

Come back.
Finish the clean.

Repeat.

The owner sometimes wondered why a few cleans took longer.

What they did not know was I was pulling double duty.

When the laundry was running…

I was tagging.

That season helped save my house.

Help save the dojo.

Get me into a reliable vehicle.

And somehow…

Still get me to Egypt.

After Egypt the lots changed.
Enforcement stopped to a halt.

FULL STOP.

The client chose not to turn them back on the way they had been before.
It is possible that chapter ended in Egypt.

Full Circle

Egypt felt different before I even arrived.

Austria had been historic.
Curacao had been magical.
Spain had been emotional.
Panama had been complicated.
Egypt felt symbolic.

Maybe it was the age of the place. Maybe it was everything life had taken to reach that point. Or maybe some part of me already knew this trip would matter more than I understood at the time.

The year itself already carried momentum.

Deadly Art of Survival Magazine had featured me in its sixteenth edition with my name appearing across all four covers. DAO has held #1 for 25 consecutive issues on Amazon.

Somewhere between survival years and rebuilding years, life had quietly started opening different doors again.
I still was not fully used to it.

When I arrived in Cairo, the scale hit immediately.

The city felt endless.

Buildings stretched in every direction while traffic moved in ways that looked impossible from the outside yet somehow continued flowing anyway.

The drive itself felt alive.
That first night carried tension.

My phone was not working correctly, I was unfamiliar with the environment, and eventually I found myself outside moving through crowded streets where I was the obvious outsider.

The smells, the noise, the movement, all of it felt completely foreign.

I remember becoming extremely aware of everything.

Eventually I returned to the hotel.

I was exhausted.

The room sat high above the city, somewhere around the ninth floor, and after everything from travel to uncertainty, I finally went to sleep.

The next morning changed everything.

I opened the curtains.

The pyramids were NOT there.

On Day 6 of 8 I ordered an Uber to get to the Pyramids of Giza and also checked out the Sphinx.

When I was at the pyramids I made several videos with the first one thanking God.

Shortly after I talked about my wife and life then onto some of the books I wrote. I spoke of my mom and how I wanted to provide for my immediate family.

After all of that emotional tension. I moved to another part of the main pyramid and made a video and I held the magazine in front of the great pyramid. One of the seven wonders of the world.

I am a supporter of DAOS for life. Plan on getting every issue X2 if not 3. so people can read about our stories.

Growing up in Alaska, I never imagined life would carry me from Beluga and Soldotna to standing in Egypt looking out toward one of the oldest wonders in human history.

Later in the day I went to the Brand New Museum in Cairo.
The museum affected me too.

There was simply too much history to absorb in one day.
Artifacts I had only seen growing up in books suddenly existed physically in front of me.

It felt overwhelming in the best possible way.
Egypt also showed another side.

Outside the tourist areas, I saw people working incredibly hard under conditions very different from what most Americans experience.

The contrast stayed with me.

It reminded me again how differently human beings experience life depending on where they are born.

Then came competition.

Joel had his own path, his own family moments, his own experiences during the trip, and I intentionally tried to give space where it was needed.

Sometimes support means stepping forward.
Sometimes it means stepping back.

That mattered to me.

One moment stayed with me.

Tom Scott had reached out to Joel.

An athlete from another world entirely seeing what Joel was doing and recognizing it.

I remember thinking how improbable all of it felt.

Years earlier we were experimenting with wheelies inside the dojo.

Now the world was paying attention.

After Egypt, life kept moving.

Joel continued doing what Joel does best: experiencing life fully.
Traveling. Exploring. Collecting experiences.

I respect that.
Because life should be lived.

As Rio approached, I stayed focused on one thing.

Support. Not pressure. Not expectations. Just support.

I asked Joel how many competitors he had.
He told me he did not want to know.
He wanted to stay focused.

I agreed immediately.

The result would arrive soon enough.

The result arrived in Rio.

Joel rolled onto the floor representing the United States.

Not Georgia, Not Tennessee, Not Chattanooga

The United States.

For nearly a decade I have watched him train.

One class. One tournament. One lesson at a time.

Now he is competing on the International Stage.

History had already been made when he became the first male wheelchair athlete named to the U.S. Karate Team.

Rio was the next chapter.

I wasn't focused on medals.
I wasn't focused on placement.

I was focused on something simpler.

Watching Joel represent the United States.

Bronze. A historic first. He won the first medal in the PKF in a wheelchair (shared) for the United States of America in Rio of May 2026.

Meanwhile another realization quietly sat in the background.

The adaptive divisions were continuing to expand.

The same systems, ideas, and advocacy work that started decades earlier were still moving.

Still growing.
Still evolving.

And now, in 2026, I found myself approaching another emotional milestone.

AAU Nationals.

Their first full National Championships with adaptive divisions officially rolling into the event structure.

Twenty years earlier I walked into Nationals with CNN following Brandon Earnshaw in that exact place. Broward County Convention Center.

Now I would walk back into Nationals again and watch adaptive divisions stand on that same stage.

That realization still overwhelms me.

Because I can see the entire timeline at once.

The first athlete.
The first experiment.
The first breakthrough.
The first U.S. Team athlete with autism.
The first male wheelchair athlete on the U.S. Team.

The survival years in between.
All of it.

And somehow I am still here.

Still teaching. Still building. Still becoming. Still experimenting.
Looking forward instead of backward.

Maybe that is the biggest lesson hidden underneath this entire story.

Life is not really about arriving.

It is about becoming.
Becoming stronger.
Becoming wiser.
Becoming more useful.

Helping other people become too.

And if this journey taught me anything, it is this:

It is never too late to reinvent yourself.

Never too late to help someone.

Never too late to become proud of yourself.

Or proud of someone else.

When the event ended July 3 2026, I walked back towards the parking lot.

Florida heat. Palm trees. Traffic moving outside the convention center.

I opened the drivers side door and turned the car over.

I rolled down the windows and let all the heat billow out of the car. The A/C is on full cold air blast mode.

Once more comfortable.

I sat in the driver's seat for a moment before leaving the lot.

Then I pulled onto the road.
Another highway.
Another season.
Another chapter waiting somewhere ahead.

And for the first time in a very long time,

I smiled driving into the unknown.

Final Reflection

The greatest lesson hidden beneath this entire journey.
For years, I thought this story was about karate.

The schools. The tournaments. The medals. The students.

But now I think karate was simply the path.
The path began long before I ever tied on a belt.

It began in a small village in Alaska with a three-year-old boy and a bear.

For most of my life, people heard that story and thought the lesson was that I survived.

I don't think that's the lesson anymore.
The lesson is what happened afterward.

Every challenge that came later was another bear.

The bullying. The failures. The empty rooms. The closed school.

The Army.
The uncertainty.
The years spent wondering if everything I had built would survive.

The truth is that life never stops putting bears in your path.

Some are bigger than others.
Some arrive when you expect them.
Most don't.

What I eventually learned is that beating the bear was never about strength.

It was about continuing.
Continuing when things were difficult.
Continuing when things were unfair.
Continuing when the outcome was uncertain.

One step.

One lesson.
One chapter at a time.

Looking across the years now, I can finally see the pattern.

The little boy survived the bear.
The bullied kid found karate.
The martial artist became a teacher.
The teacher became a mentor.
And somewhere along the way, I became a student again.

Learning the same lesson life had been teaching me from the very beginning.

Keep going.

Because it is never too late to reinvent yourself.

Never too late to help someone.

Never too late to become proud of who you are.

Or proud of someone else.

The story is not over.

Not for me.
Not for the students whose lives crossed mine.
Not for the people still fighting their own bears.

The most improbable part of this journey may not be everything that has already happened.

It may be everything that comes next.

Be ready for the next bear.

It's coming.

One Final Discovery

While assembling Improbable, I made one final discovery.

For years, a newspaper article and news story reported that history had been made five times during the 2012 season.

Only while reviewing the accomplishments for this book did I realize the number was actually eight. Furthermore I didn't realize it was 23 until my final edits as well.

Several barriers had been grouped together. Others had never been counted separately.

What appeared in print as five pieces of history was, in reality, eight separate barriers being broken.

The interesting part is that I wasn't keeping score.

I wasn't focused on making history.

I was focused on helping people.

Only years later did I fully appreciate the scope of what had occurred. The medals, qualifications, and officiating milestones were never the goal. They were evidence of what can happen when people are given a place to belong, an opportunity to grow, and someone willing to believe in them long before the rest of the world does.

Green's Karate has made U.S. Karate History 23 Times

Over the years, people often asked me why I fought so hard to keep Green's Karate alive.

The answer was never the building.

It was never the trophies.
It was never the business.
It was the people.

Looking back, these are some of the moments that became part of U.S. karate history.

Green's Karate students have made U.S. karate history 23 times

2006

1. First person with autism to qualify and compete in the U.S. Karate Nationals non-handicap division.

Brandon Earnshaw

2010

2. First female with autism to qualify and compete in the U.S. Karate Nationals non-handicap division.

Katie Dietsche

2012

3. First blind female to qualify for the U.S. Karate Nationals non-handicap division.

Katie Whipple

4. First blind female to win a medal in the U.S. Karate Nationals non-handicap division.

Ryan Rogers

5. First person with autism to win a medal in the U.S. Karate Nationals non-handicap division against able-bodied competitors.
6. First person with autism to win a medal in kata in the U.S. Karate Nationals non-handicap division.
7. First person with autism to win a medal in kumite in the U.S. Karate Nationals non-handicap division.
8. First person with autism to officiate at the U.S. Karate National Championships.
9. First person with autism to become a USANKF Kata Judge.
10. First person with autism to become a USANKF Kumite Judge.

2013

Ryan Rogers

11. First person with autism to win a medal in the Men's 18–34 Intermediate Kumite Division at the U.S. Karate Nationals non-handicap division.

2015

Ryan Rogers

12. First person with autism to compete in a non-handicap weapons division at the U.S. Karate Nationals.
13. First person with autism to compete in the Men's 18–34 Advanced Kata Division. (Shared History)
14. First person with autism to compete in the Men's 18–34 Advanced Kumite Division. (Shared History)

2016

Ryan Rogers

15. First athlete with autism in America named to the U.S. Karate Team.
16. First American with autism to compete in the WKF World Karate Championships.

Ryan Rogers – Linz, Austria (2016)

2017

17. First American with autism to win a medal in international karate competition. Silver

Ryan Rogers – PKF Championships, Curaçao (2017)

2025

Joel Westbrook

18. First male wheelchair athlete named to the U.S. Karate Team (Para).
19. First male wheelchair karate athlete from the United States to compete at the WKF Karate World Championships.

Joel Westbrook – Cairo, Egypt (2025)

2026

20. First male wheelchair athlete to become a USANKF Kata Judge.
Joel Westbrook
21. First male wheelchair athlete to become a USANKF Kumite Judge.
Joel Westbrook
22. First male wheelchair athlete to compete in a PKF for the United States (shared history).
23. First male wheelchair athlete to win a medal at the PKF Bronze, (shared history).

Joel Westbrook - Rio, Brazil (2026)

Special Thanks:

God, my wife Michelle Young, my parents, Randy and Rebecca Bishop and brothers Hyatt, Brian and Derek, my Sensei, Tanaka Sensei, Sensei Nathan Ingram, Grand master George Chung, Master Jeff Warton, Senpai Logan Blakeley, Senpai David Brady, Senpai Greg Carson, Senpai Ryan Rogers, Pam Germain, Wendy Westbrook, Craig Westbrook, Senpai Joel Westbrook, Sensei Eric Rossini, Sensei Bobby Carter, Delphin Labrador, Jose Garcia, Paden, Powell, Singleton, all my drill sergeants, Senpai Katie Dietsche, Senpai Katie Whipple, Senpai Brandon Earnshaw, Mac Geer, Senpai Tejit Pamidi, Senpai Jim Hibbs, Senpai Sonny Ravinder, Senpai Jude Rifai, Sensei Bryan Ratliff, Jericho Aguayo, Aaron Messengill, Senpai Eltoran Ball, Senpai Cameron Ball, Senpai Doug Daugtherty, Keith Sandoval, Sensei Tamara Canedo, Sensei and Coach Jeffery Kohn, Karate Can-Do Foundation, Sasha Garretison, Jan Bobek, Tess Jelasic, Mr. Musson, Mrs. Quelette, Mr. Simons, Mr. Blankenship, Dr. Anz, Dr. Baleerio, Dr. Nguyen, Memorial Hospital X3, Lee Waters, Piper, Cheryl, Maria, SGT MAJ Magwood, Major Weber, Tina Starr, Dawn Blaylock, Glynn Hodges, Joe Weiless, Ali Jones, Kyle Saylors, Kenny Saylors, Senpai Linda Weimer, Senpai Eric Jones, Ernest Long, The Van Dolson Family, Lee Junior, Dennis Tate, Sensei Shawn Masters, Ted O'donnel, Bob Allen, Jolene Brown,Helene Mann (Schoolcraft) Sarah Stephens, Dan Smith, Daniel Smith, Aaron Hecht, Patrick Moran, Berry Goatley, Chris Clift, Spring Larrow, Suresh Manuel, Sensei Brody Burns, Joy Giles, Tina Attlee, Sensei Michael Buttermark, Alina Earnshaw, Trish Cox, Grace Perrry Callahan, Christopher Hodgin, John Rescober ,Molly Blakeley, Ryan Netusil, Deborah Duncan, Sensei Nader Azzouzi, Sensei Stephanie Buckner, Sensei Samantha Hostettler, Sensei Guillemet's, Sensei Jimmy Blann, Dawn Brown, Andrea Harkins, Emil Martirossian, Ryan Thomas, Ryan Howard, Stuart Hoover, Sensei Cedric Barksdale, Sabahudin Tricic, Sensei Mark Lingl, Sensei John Klatt, Sensei Miguel Ochoa, Chantal Starr, Jen Falbey, Property Preppers, Mary Truesdale, Adam Older, Sensei Teresa Hicks, Robert C. Baker, Heather Attlee, John Lathim, Julie Cooley, Joey Dockery, James Mullis, Juan Peters, Skip, Beverly and James Dove.

No memoir can fully capture every person who shaped a life.

Along this journey there were teachers, students, friends, competitors, officials, coworkers, family members, supporters, and even critics who influenced the path in ways both large and small.

Some appear by name in these pages. Many do not.

That omission is not a measure of importance.

A life spanning nearly five decades cannot fit every story, every conversation, every lesson, or every act of kindness into a single book.

To those whose names were not mentioned but who influence was felt, please know that your contribution mattered.

You helped shap the person who wrote these pages.

For that I am grateful.

About the Author

Corey Green is the founder and owner of Green's Karate in Chattanooga, Tennessee, where he has taught martial arts since 2003. He began his teaching career in Alaska in 1997 and opened his first martial arts school in 1998 with a $1,500 signature loan and a dream.

Over the past four decades, Corey has trained in traditional martial arts, coached athletes at the national and international levels, served as a referee and instructor for USA Karate, and helped create opportunities for athletes with disabilities to compete and succeed.

His students have made U.S. karate history twenty-one times, including producing America's first athlete with autism on the U.S. Karate Team and the first male wheelchair athlete on the U.S. Karate Team.

Outside the dojo, Corey has worked as PBS host, event organizer, referee, entrepreneur, rideshare driver and advocate. Through every success and setback, he has remained committed to helping others discover confidence, discipline, and purpose through martial arts.

Improbable is his first memoir.

He lives in Tennessee with his wife and two dogs Lucy and Luna and continues to teach, mentor, write, and build new projects while preparing for whatever bear comes next.

IMPROBABLE
THE STORY OF
COREY GREEN
and GREEN'S KARATE
TEAM
USA
COREY GREEN

Made in the USA
Coppell, TX
24 June 2026

83016951R00174